BETTER HOMES AND GARDENS®

Gas Grill
COOKBOOK

BETTER HOMES AND GARDENS® BOOKS
Des Moines, Iowa

BETTER HOMES AND GARDENS® BOOKS
An Imprint of Meredith® Books
President, Book Group: Joseph J. Ward
Vice President and Editorial Director: Elizabeth P. Rice
Managing Editor: Christopher Cavanaugh
Executive Editor: Nancy N. Green
Art Director: Ernest Shelton
Test Kitchen Director: Sharon Stilwell

GAS GRILL COOKBOOK
Editor: Shelli McConnell
Contributing Editor: Linda J. Henry
Graphic Designer: Lynda Haupert
Production Editor: Paula Forest
Test Kitchen Product Supervisor: Marilyn Cornelius
Food Stylist: Janet Pittman
Cover Photographer: Mike Dieter

On the cover: Baby Back Ribs with Mustard Sauce
(page 32) and Grilled Mixed Veggies (page 123)

WE CARE!

All of us at Better Homes and Gardens® Books are dedicated
to providing you with the information and ideas you need to
create tasty foods. We welcome your comments and suggestions.
Write us at: Better Homes and Gardens® Books,
Cookbook Editorial Department, RW240, 1716 Locust Street,
Des Moines, IA 50309-3023

If you would like to order additional copies of any of our books,
call 1-800-678-2803 or check with your local bookstore.

Our seal assures you that every recipe in *Gas Grill Cookbook*
has been tested in the Better Homes and Gardens® Test Kitchen.
This means that each recipe is practical and reliable, and meets
our high standards of taste appeal. We guarantee your satisfaction
with this book for as long as you own it.

Contents

Introduction

It's time to take the guesswork out of gas grilling. And it's time to start using that gas grill for more than an occasional steak or handful of franks.

This book is *hot!* It sizzles with recipes for all your barbecue occasions—from a lazy afternoon picnic at the park to a sunset dinner. And it's overflowing with recipes for ribs dripping with sauce, old- and new-fangled burgers, juicy chicken, and much more.

You'll find more than 80 main dish recipes developed specifically for and tested on gas grills. You'll also find everything to complete your meal, from appetizers and side dishes to desserts. In addition, you'll run across lots of useful information, including the difference between direct and indirect grilling; using your gas grill safely; how to save time by combining microwave cooking and grilling; and how to prevent flare-ups on your gas grill.

With this book and these recipes, you'll most certainly wow your family and friends with your gas grilling know-how!

Grill Basics

Whether you're a gas grilling beginner or a well-seasoned pro, the next few pages are full of invaluable information. Learn some important gas grilling safety tips, all about direct and indirect cooking, and how the itsy, bitsy spider can wreak havoc on your next grill-out!

In This Chapter:

Grill Basics

Types of Gas Grills

Today's gas grills are available in all shapes and sizes, catering to every taste and pocketbook. They range from portable tabletop varieties with disposable Liquid Propane (L.P.) cylinders to elaborate wagons complete with cutting boards, range-style side burners for heating sauces and side dishes, and sometimes even insulated coolers for keeping food and drinks hot or cold. You can pick from single-burner, 2-burner, and 3-burner gas grills. (One note about tabletop gas grills: Whatever you grill cannot exceed $3\frac{1}{4}$ inches in height or the cover will not fit on the grill.)

Gas grills fueled by refillable propane tanks usually roll on wheels, making them easy to move around the yard. Natural gas units, however, are often mounted on a fixed pedestal connected to permanent gas lines underneath the lawn.

Some gas grills are lined with ceramic briquettes or volcanic lava rock, while others have heat-conducting metal bars. Whatever your gas grill comes equipped with, the theory is the same—juices drip onto the briquettes, lava rock, or metal bars creating the smoke that gives foods that irresistible barbecued flavor. (Charcoal-flavored briquettes for gas grills are now available. Check with your gas grill manufacturer before using these briquettes, though.)

Lighting Your Gas Grill

Grab your fork...get set...go! Gas grilling is that simple and that fast. There's never any guessing about how many charcoal briquettes to use, never any waiting 20 to 30 minutes for the coals to get hot, and finally, never any debate about whether the coals are hot enough.

Before starting your gas grill, open the lid and turn all the burner control knobs to OFF. Next, turn the gas on at the source. From this point, you should refer to your owner's manual for specific lighting instructions. The procedures vary a little depending on whether you have a match lighting grill, a push button ignitor, or an electronic ignitor. After lighting your grill, close the lid and preheat the grill on HIGH for 10 to 15 minutes. Again, follow your owner's manual recommendations for preheating.

▬▬ Cooking with Your Gas Grill

The recipes in this book are grilled by using either direct or indirect cooking—and many of the recipes include directions for both.

Direct Cooking

The direct cooking method means to place the food on the grill directly over the fire. It's a faster cooking method because more intense heat is provided and allows for more browning on the outside of foods. The food must be turned during grilling to cook on both sides. For the best results, turn only once, halfway through grilling. Frequent turning can dry out meat and even cause burgers to crumble. We like to use direct cooking for foods that have a relatively short cooking time, such as burgers and fish, and/or foods with a low fat content, such as well-trimmed steaks and chops.

Indirect Cooking

In this method, food is cooked by hot air circulating around the food, much like a convection oven. It's a slower cooking method because less heat is provided. And since there is less heat, flare-ups from dripping foods are minimized. You'll use indirect cooking for larger cuts of meat, such as roasts, and for foods with sugary sauces, glazes, or marinades.

Refer to your owner's manual for specific directions on indirect cooking. Usually, if you have a 2-burner gas grill, after preheating with both burners on, you'll turn off one burner and place the food over the unlit side, away from the heat source. For 3-burner gas grills, you'll usually turn off the middle burner after preheating and place the food in the center of the grill. And for single-burner gas grills, after preheating, the burner is usually turned down to LOW.

How Hot is Hot?

You'll need to be able to judge how hot the heat is coming from your grill, because not all foods are grilled at the same temperature. Hold your hand, palm side down, where your food will cook and at the same height as the food will be grilled. Count by saying, "one thousand-one, one thousand-two..." for each second you can hold your hand there. You'll need to remove your hand after 2 seconds for high heat, 3 seconds for medium-high heat, 4 seconds for medium heat, 5 seconds for medium-low heat, and 6 seconds for low heat.

Special Gas Grill Safety Tips

Today, with more people lighting up gas grills than ever before, it's important to remember that a successful barbecue is a safe barbecue. All gas grill manufacturers have specific instruction manuals and warnings as to proper use. Follow these instructions and pay attention to the warnings; failure to do so can result in voiding your warranty, or worse, damage to property and/or personal injury. The following list of tips will help make your grilling safe and trouble free.

■ Always read your owner's manual before using a new gas grill and especially before igniting it for the first time.

■ Follow the detailed instructions that are packed with your gas grill for specific assembly procedures. Improper assembly of a new gas grill can be dangerous.

■ Gas grills are manufactured to either operate on liquid propane or natural gas. Never attempt to operate your grill on gases other than the type specified for your particular grill.

■ Never use your gas grill indoors; they are designed for outdoor use only.

■ When not in use, your L.P. tank valve should be turned off and the grill must be kept outside in a well-ventilated area. If you store your gas grill indoors, the L.P. tank must be disconnected, removed, and stored outdoors.

■ Never store the L.P. tank in a place where temperatures can reach 125° F.

■ Transport and store your L.P. tank in an upright position.

■ Do not store or use gasoline or other combustible or flammable materials or liquids near your gas grill.

■ Do not lean over your gas grill when igniting the burners.

■ Do not attempt to move a gas grill when the burners are ignited or the grill is hot.

■ Always make sure the grill hood is open before lighting your gas grill.

■ Do not cover your gas grill while it is still warm.

■ If a burner doesn't ignite, turn off the gas. Keep the grill hood open and wait five minutes before trying again.

The Itsy Bitsy Spider

Spiders, because they're attracted to an additive placed in gas (especially natural gas), can cause some real problems for you and your gas grill. This additive, plus the fact that the venturi tube is a narrow, dark, protected area, makes the burner attractive to spiders and other insects for spinning webs or building nests.

If you suddenly develop problems in lighting your gas grill or experience "FLASH-BACK" (fire at the air inlet hole of the venturi tube), spiders are probably the culprit. But getting rid of the spider webs blocking the venturi tube is as quick as reciting the Itsy Bitsy Spider. Just insert a small bottle brush or long pipe cleaner into the end of the burner and twist and pull back and forth several times. Be sure the gas is turned off before you do the cleaning. See your owner's manual for more information about the venturi tube.

Healthful Grilling

Perhaps you've read research findings that suggest some compounds formed during grilling are potentially hazardous. These substances are caused by excessive smoke coming from fat flare-ups. The Barbecue Industry Association recommends using indirect cooking if you have concerns about these health risks. By using the indirect cooking method for gas grills, the fat drips onto an unlit burner, preventing these flare-ups. To date, no government, health, or research organization has recommended eliminating grilling as a cooking method. But because of these concerns, we have included both indirect and direct grilling methods in our recipes wherever possible.

Cleaning Your Gas Grill

As with any appliance, some simple maintenance will add years to the life of your gas grill and keep it looking great.

1. Wipe the inside and outside surfaces of the grill with a soft cloth and warm, soapy water. Rinse with clear water and wipe dry.

2. Prevent grease build-up by wiping the inside of the lid with paper towels while it's still warm.

3. After every use, turn your grill on HIGH for 10 to 15 minutes (with the lid closed); turn off. Then loosen residue from the grill rack with a brass bristle brush. This not only helps prevent sticking, but also avoids flare-ups.

4. Check your owner's manual for cleaning tips and specific manufacturer's cleaning instructions for all other grill parts.

Put It in a Bun

Here's a bonanza of grilling favorites—burgers, franks, and brats—all serve-on-a-bun specialties for everyday and every occasion. You just can't beat this lip-smacking collection of "fun in a bun" entrees.

In This Chapter:

All-American Burgers

2 tablespoons fine dry bread crumbs	4 slices Monterey Jack cheese
2 tablespoons catsup	4 slices Colby cheese
1 tablespoon prepared mustard	4 lettuce leaves
¼ teaspoon onion powder	4 hamburger buns, split and toasted
⅛ teaspoon pepper	4 thin onion slices
1 pound lean ground beef	4 thin tomato slices

Serve these thick, juicy burgers with potato chips, pickles, and fresh fruit for a quick summer supper.

1 In a medium mixing bowl combine bread crumbs, catsup, and mustard. Stir in onion powder and pepper. Add ground beef; mix well. Shape meat mixture into four ¾-inch-thick patties.

2 Preheat gas grill. Adjust heat for direct cooking. Place patties on grill rack over medium heat. Cover and grill for 14 to 18 minutes or till no pink remains, turning once halfway through. Top each patty with one slice of Monterey Jack cheese and one slice of Colby cheese for the last 2 minutes of grilling.

3 Serve patties on lettuce-lined buns with onion and tomato slices. Makes 4 servings.

Indirect Grilling: Preheat gas grill. Adjust heat for indirect cooking. Place patties on grill rack over medium heat. Cover and grill for 20 to 24 minutes or till no pink remains, turning once halfway through. Continue as directed above.

Per serving: 529 calories, 36 g protein, 29 g carbohydrate, 30 g total fat (14 g saturated), 110 mg cholesterol, 719 mg sodium, 512 mg potassium

Firecracker Burgers

These double-decker burgers really live up to their name. They're seasoned with green chili peppers and ground red pepper, then topped with hot pepper cheese.

1 pound lean ground beef
1 4-ounce can diced green chili peppers, drained
⅛ teaspoon ground red pepper
4 slices cheddar cheese with peppers or Monterey Jack cheese with jalapeño peppers

4 hamburger buns, split and toasted
4 thin tomato slices
4 thin red onion slices
¼ cup buttermilk ranch salad dressing or creamy cucumber salad dressing

1 In a medium mixing bowl combine ground beef, chili peppers, and red pepper; mix well. Shape meat mixture into eight ¼-inch-thick patties.

2 Preheat gas grill. Adjust heat for direct cooking. Place patties on grill rack over medium heat. Cover and grill for 7 to 9 minutes or till no pink remains, turning once halfway through. Top 4 of the patties with a cheese slice for the last 2 minutes of grilling.

3 Place one patty with cheese on each bun. Top with a tomato slice, a plain patty, an onion slice, and salad dressing. Makes 4 servings.

Indirect Grilling: Preheat gas grill. Adjust heat for indirect cooking. Place patties on grill rack over medium heat. Cover and grill for 10 to 12 minutes or till no pink remains, turning once halfway through. Continue as directed above.

Per serving: 529 calories, 32 g protein, 23 g carbohydrate, 33 g total fat (13 g saturated), 105 mg cholesterol, 727 mg sodium, 375 mg potassium

Sour Cream and Herb Burgers

1 beaten egg
¼ cup fine dry bread crumbs
¼ cup dairy sour cream
1 teaspoon snipped fresh thyme or ¼ teaspoon dried thyme, crushed
1 teaspoon snipped fresh rosemary or ¼ teaspoon dried rosemary, crushed
1 teaspoon snipped fresh parsley
¼ teaspoon salt
⅛ teaspoon pepper
1 pound lean ground beef
¼ cup alfalfa sprouts
4 whole wheat hamburger buns, split and toasted
4 tomato slices
¼ cup dairy sour cream (optional)

Save yourself a few grams of fat by using one of the "light" sour creams that are available.

1 In a medium mixing bowl combine egg, bread crumbs, ¼ cup sour cream, thyme, rosemary, parsley, salt, and pepper. Add ground beef; mix well. Shape meat mixture into four ¾-inch-thick patties.

2 Preheat gas grill. Adjust heat for direct cooking. Place patties on grill rack over medium heat. Cover and grill for 14 to 18 minutes or till no pink remains, turning once halfway through.

3 Serve on alfalfa sprout-lined buns. Top with tomato slices and, if desired, remaining sour cream. Makes 4 servings.

Indirect Grilling: Preheat gas grill. Adjust heat for indirect cooking. Place patties on a grill rack over medium heat. Cover and grill for 20 to 24 minutes or till no pink remains, turning once halfway through. Continue as directed above.

Per serving: 376 calories, 28 g protein, 23 g carbohydrate, 19 g total fat (8 g saturated), 130 mg cholesterol, 446 mg sodium, 490 mg potassium

5-Spice Pork Burgers with Plum Sauce

1 beaten egg
¼ cup fine dry bread crumbs
2 tablespoons finely chopped onion
2 tablespoons soy sauce
½ to ¾ teaspoon five-spice powder

⅛ teaspoon garlic salt
1 pound lean ground pork
  Chinese cabbage leaves
4 hamburger buns, split and toasted
4 tablespoons plum sauce

1 In a medium mixing bowl combine egg, bread crumbs, onion, soy sauce, five-spice powder, and garlic salt. Add ground pork; mix well. Shape meat mixture into four ¾-inch-thick patties.

2 Preheat gas grill. Adjust heat for direct cooking. Place patties on grill rack over medium heat. Cover and grill for 14 to 18 minutes or till juices run clear, turning once halfway through.

3 Serve on cabbage-lined buns with plum sauce. Makes 4 servings.

Indirect Grilling: Preheat gas grill. Adjust heat for indirect cooking. Place patties on grill rack over medium heat. Cover and grill for 20 to 24 minutes or till juices run clear, turning once halfway through. Continue as directed above.

Per serving: 327 calories, 22 g protein, 33 g carbohydrate, 13 g total fat (1 g saturated), 106 mg cholesterol, 880 mg sodium, 337 mg potassium

Mustard-Glazed Pork Burgers

1 pound lean ground pork or
  ground beef
1 teaspoon snipped fresh sage
  or ¼ teaspoon dried sage
  leaves, crushed
¼ teaspoon salt
⅛ teaspoon pepper
2 tablespoons brown mustard

1 tablespoon corn syrup
1 teaspoon margarine or
  butter, melted
1 8¼-ounce can pineapple
  slices, drained
4 hamburger buns, split and
  toasted

1 In a medium mixing bowl combine ground pork or beef, sage, salt, and pepper; mix well. Shape meat mixture into four ¾-inch-thick patties.

2 Preheat gas grill. Adjust heat for direct cooking. Place patties on grill rack over medium heat. Cover and grill for 14 to 18 minutes or till juices run clear, turning once halfway through.

3 Meanwhile, for glaze, in a small mixing bowl combine mustard, corn syrup, and margarine or butter. Place pineapple slices atop patties during the last minute of grilling; brush with glaze. Serve on buns. Makes 4 servings.

Indirect Grilling: Preheat gas grill. Adjust heat for indirect cooking. Place patties on a grill rack over medium heat. Cover and grill for 20 to 24 minutes or till juices run clear, turning once halfway through. Continue as directed above.

Per serving: 290 calories, 18 g protein, 27 g carbohydrate, 12 g total fat (1 g saturated), 53 mg cholesterol, 532 mg sodium, 286 mg potassium

Cajun Pork Burgers

If you're a real lover of hot and spicy food, use hot-style pork sausage in these special burgers.

½ **pound lean ground pork**
½ **pound bulk pork sausage**
1 **teaspoon Cajun seasoning***
4 **lettuce leaves**

4 **hamburger buns, split and toasted**
4 **thin tomato slices**

1 In a medium mixing bowl combine ground pork, sausage, and Cajun seasoning; mix well. Shape mixture into four ¾-inch-thick patties.

2 Preheat gas grill. Adjust heat for direct cooking. Place patties on grill rack over medium heat. Cover and grill for 14 to 18 minutes or till juices run clear, turning once halfway through.

3 Serve on lettuce-lined buns with tomato slices. Makes 4 servings.

***Note:** To make your own Cajun seasoning, in a container with a tight-fitting lid combine 1 tablespoon *salt*, 2 teaspoons *ground red pepper*, 1 teaspoon *ground white pepper*, 1 teaspoon *garlic powder*, and 1 teaspoon *ground black pepper*. Store, covered, at room temperature. Makes about 3 tablespoons.

Indirect Grilling: Preheat gas grill. Adjust heat for indirect cooking. Place patties on grill rack over medium heat. Cover and grill for 20 to 24 minutes or till no pink remains, turning once halfway through. Continue as directed above.

Per serving: 291 calories, 16 g protein, 23 g carbohydrate, 15 g total fat (3 g saturated), 49 mg cholesterol, 612 mg sodium, 305 mg potassium

Gyro Burgers

1 beaten egg
¼ cup fine dry bread crumbs
2 tablespoons plain yogurt
1 clove garlic, minced
¼ teaspoon salt
¼ teaspoon ground cumin
⅛ teaspoon pepper

1 pound lean ground lamb or
   ground beef
2 large pita bread rounds, split
   crosswise
¼ cup plain yogurt
12 thin cucumber slices
1 medium tomato, chopped

1 In a medium mixing bowl combine egg, bread crumbs, the 2 table-spoons yogurt, garlic, salt, cumin, and pepper. Add ground lamb or beef; mix well. Shape meat mixture into four ¾-inch-thick patties.

2 Preheat gas grill. Adjust heat for direct cooking. Place patties on grill rack over medium heat. Cover and grill for 14 to 18 minutes or till no pink remains, turning once halfway through.

3 Serve in pita halves with the ¼ cup yogurt, cucumber slices, and chopped tomato. Makes 4 servings.

Indirect Grilling: Preheat gas grill. Adjust heat for indirect cooking. Place patties on grill rack over medium heat. Cover and grill for 20 to 24 minutes or till no pink remains, turning once halfway through. Continue as directed above.

Per serving: 341 calories, 25 g protein, 20 g carbohydrate, 17 g total fat (7 g saturated), 129 mg cholesterol, 386 mg sodium, 497 mg potassium

Capture the flavor of the Greek specialty, gyros (yee rohs), with these quick and easy burgers.

Feta-Stuffed Lamb Burgers

A glaze of melted apple jelly spiced with a touch of cinnamon tops these Greek burgers.

1 pound lean ground lamb
1½ teaspoons snipped fresh mint or ½ teaspoon dried mint, crushed
¼ teaspoon salt
⅛ teaspoon ground coriander
⅓ cup finely crumbled feta cheese

¼ cup apple jelly
1 tablespoon lemon juice
⅛ teaspoon ground cinnamon
2 large whole wheat pita bread rounds, split crosswise
2 cups shredded spinach

1 In a medium mixing bowl combine ground lamb, mint, salt, and coriander; mix well. Shape meat mixture into eight ¼-inch-thick patties.

2 Place feta cheese in centers of 4 of the patties. Top with remaining patties; press edges to seal.

3 Preheat gas grill. Adjust heat for direct cooking. Place patties on grill rack over medium heat. Cover and grill for 14 to 18 minutes or till no pink remains, turning once halfway through.

4 Meanwhile, for glaze, in a small saucepan combine apple jelly, lemon juice, and cinnamon; heat and stir till jelly melts. Brush glaze over patties during the last minute of grilling.

5 Serve in pita halves with spinach. Makes 4 servings.

Indirect Grilling: Preheat gas grill. Adjust heat for indirect cooking. Place patties on grill rack over medium heat. Cover and grill for 20 to 24 minutes or till no pink remains, turning once halfway through. Continue as directed above.

Per serving: 384 calories, 25 g protein, 26 g carbohydrate, 20 g total fat (10 g saturated), 94 mg cholesterol, 528 mg sodium, 516 mg potassium

Curried Turkey Burgers

2 tablespoons thinly sliced
green onion
1½ teaspoons curry powder
2 teaspoons margarine or
butter
1 teaspoon all-purpose flour
¾ cup plain yogurt
1 beaten egg
¼ cup fine dry bread crumbs

¼ teaspoon salt
⅛ teaspoon pepper
1 pound ground raw turkey or
ground raw chicken
2 tablespoons finely chopped
chutney
4 kaiser rolls or hamburger
buns, split and toasted

1 For curry sauce, in a small saucepan cook green onion and curry powder in margarine or butter till onion is tender. Remove from heat. Stir flour into yogurt; stir into onion mixture.

2 In a medium mixing bowl combine egg and 2 tablespoons of the curry sauce. Stir in bread crumbs, salt, and pepper. Add ground turkey or chicken; mix well. Shape mixture into four ¾-inch-thick patties.

3 Preheat gas grill. Adjust heat for direct cooking. Place patties on grill rack over medium heat. Cover and grill for 14 to 18 minutes or till juices run clear, turning once halfway through.

4 Meanwhile, stir chutney into remaining curry sauce. Cook and stir just till heated through (do not boil).

5 Serve on buns with curry sauce. Makes 4 servings.

Indirect Grilling: Preheat gas grill. Adjust heat for indirect cooking. Place meat on grill rack over medium heat. Cover and grill for 20 to 24 minutes or till juices run clear, turning once halfway through. Continue as directed above.

Per serving: 248 calories, 20 g protein, 14 g carbohydrate, 12 g total fat (3 g saturated), 96 mg cholesterol, 303 mg sodium, 324 mg potassium

Pizza Dogs for Kids

4 frankfurters
4 hamburger buns, split and
    toasted
½ cup shredded mozzarella
    cheese (2 ounces)

2 to 3 tablespoons pizza
    sauce, heated
2 thinly sliced green onions
    (optional)

1 Make 4 small cuts crosswise on 1 side of each frankfurter, cutting to, but not through, the opposite side. Curl ends around to meet and fasten with a wooden toothpick.

2 Preheat gas grill. Adjust heat for direct cooking. Place frankfurters on grill rack over medium-high heat. Cover and grill for 5 to 7 minutes or till heated through.

3 Remove toothpicks. Place frankfurters on toasted buns. Fill centers with cheese; top with pizza sauce, and, if desired, green onions. Serves 4.

Per serving: *337 calories, 13 g protein, 23 g carbohydrate, 21 g total fat (8 g saturated), 37 mg cholesterol, 987 mg sodium, 171 mg potassium*

Hot Diggity Dogs!

Next time you need a special summertime menu for a group of grade schoolers, here's an idea that's sure to please.

Cut, curl, and grill frankfurters as directed in the recipe above. Then set up an assortment of toppers and let the kids fill their hot dog rings with whatever they choose.

Some of the toppers you might want to offer include baked beans, potato salad, coleslaw, pickle relish, pickles, canned chili (heat it up first), mustard, catsup, and some melted cheese spread.

And hey, because grown-ups like hot dogs, too, you could offer some more "sophisticated" toppers such as jalapeño pepper rings, chopped sweet peppers, and sliced olives for any adults in your group.

Deluxe Franks with BBQ Sauce

1 **8-ounce can tomato sauce**
¼ **cup chopped onion**
1 **tablespoon coarse-grain brown mustard**
1 **teaspoon sugar**
1 **teaspoon lemon juice**
¼ **teaspoon garlic powder**

8 **frankfurters**
8 **2½ x ¼-inch strips American or cheddar cheese**
8 **slices bacon**
8 **frankfurter buns, split and toasted**

1 For sauce, in a medium saucepan combine tomato sauce, onion, mustard, sugar, lemon juice, and garlic powder. Bring to boiling. Reduce heat and simmer, covered, about 15 minutes or till onion is tender. Remove from heat; set aside.

2 Slice frankfurters lengthwise, cutting to, but not through, the opposite side to make a pocket. Place one strip of cheese in each pocket.

3 In a skillet cook bacon till nearly done but not crisp. Wrap one slice of bacon around each filled frankfurter.

4 Preheat gas grill. Adjust heat for direct cooking. Place frankfurters, cheese side up, on grill rack over medium-high heat. Cover and grill for 8 to 10 minutes or till bacon is cooked and frankfurters are heated through, turning occasionally.

5 To serve, dip franks in sauce and place in buns. Serve with remaining sauce. Makes 8 servings.

Per serving: 361 calories, 13 g protein, 25 g carbohydrate, 23 g total fat (8 g saturated), 38 mg cholesterol, 1,228 mg sodium, 286 mg potassium

Sausage and Peperonata Sandwiches

Peperonata is an Italian mixture of sweet peppers, onion, and garlic cooked in olive oil. It's served hot as a condiment with meats or cold as an antipasto.

4 fresh hot or mild Italian sausage links (¾ to 1 pound)

4 hoagie buns, split and toasted Peperonata

1 Use a fork to pierce several holes in the skin of each sausage link. Preheat gas grill. Adjust heat for indirect cooking. Place sausage links on grill rack over medium heat. Cover and grill for 20 to 25 minutes or till sausage juices run clear, turning once halfway through. Serve sausages on buns. Spoon Peperonata over sausages. Makes 4 servings.

Peperonata: In a large skillet cook and stir 1 small *onion*, thinly sliced and separated into rings; 2 cloves *garlic*, minced; 1 tablespoon snipped *fresh oregano* or 1 teaspoon *dried oregano*, crushed; and ½ teaspoon *salt* in 2 tablespoons *olive oil* till onion is tender. Stir in one 7-ounce jar (½ cup) roasted sweet red peppers, drained and cut into strips, and 3 tablespoons sliced pitted ripe olives; heat through.

Per serving: 676 calories, 25 g protein, 80 g carbohydrate, 28 g total fat (8 g saturated), 49 mg cholesterol, 1,635 mg sodium, 410 mg potassium

Brats in Beer with Kraut Relish

6 fresh (uncooked) bratwursts
2 12-ounce cans (3 cups) beer
12 whole black peppercorns

6 bratwurst or frankfurter buns,
    split and toasted
Coarse-grain brown mustard
Kraut Relish

1 Pierce several holes in the skin of each bratwurst. In a large saucepan combine bratwursts, beer, and peppercorns. Bring to boiling. Reduce heat and simmer, covered, about 20 minutes or till brats are no longer pink. Drain.

2 Preheat gas grill. Adjust heat for direct cooking. Place brats on grill rack over medium-high heat. Cover and grill for 7 to 8 minutes or till skins are golden, turning frequently.

3 Serve brats on buns with mustard. Using a slotted spoon, spoon Kraut Relish over brats. Makes 6 servings.

Kraut Relish: In a small saucepan combine ¼ cup *vinegar* and 3 tablespoons *brown sugar*. Bring to boiling, stirring just till sugar dissolves. Cool. In a medium mixing bowl combine one 8-ounce can *sauerkraut*, drained; ¼ cup finely chopped *sweet red or green pepper*; 2 tablespoons sliced *green onion*; and 1 teaspoon *caraway seed*. Stir vinegar mixture into sauerkraut mixture. Cover and chill for several hours or overnight, stirring occasionally. Serve at room temperature.

Per serving: 676 calories, 22 g protein, 82 g carbohydrate, 27 g total fat (1 g saturated), 0 mg cholesterol, 1,504 mg sodium, 201 mg potassium

Roasted Pepper and Steak Sandwiches

Scoring your flank steak shortens the meat fibers, making them more tender. It also allows more of the marinade to soak in.

1 1- to 1½-pound beef flank steak
½ cup clear Italian salad dressing
⅓ cup dry red or white wine
3 tablespoons thinly sliced green onion
2 tablespoons soy sauce
2 cloves garlic, minced
    Several dashes bottled hot pepper sauce
1 medium sweet red pepper
1 medium sweet green pepper
1 tablespoon olive oil or cooking oil
4 individual French-style rolls, split and toasted

1 Score meat by making shallow cuts at 1-inch intervals diagonally across steak in a diamond pattern. Repeat scoring on second side. Place meat in a plastic bag set in a shallow dish. For marinade, combine salad dressing, wine, green onion, soy sauce, garlic, and hot pepper sauce. Pour marinade over steak. Close bag. Marinate in refrigerator for 6 to 24 hours, turning occasionally.

2 Quarter the peppers lengthwise. Remove the stems, seeds, and membranes. Brush skins with olive oil. Preheat gas grill. Adjust heat for direct cooking. Place peppers on grill rack over medium-low heat, skin side down, perpendicular to grill rack so pieces don't fall through. Cover and grill about 15 minutes or till crisp-tender and lightly charred. Immediately place pepper pieces in a clean brown paper bag. Close bag tightly; cool. Peel cooled peppers with a sharp knife. Cut into bite-size strips. Set aside.

3 Drain steak, reserving marinade. Place steak on grill rack over medium heat. Cover and grill for 18 to 22 minutes or till desired doneness, turning once and brushing occasionally with remaining marinade. Do not brush with marinade during the last 5 minutes of grilling; discard any remaining marinade.

4 To serve, slice steak diagonally across the grain into very thin slices. Pile steak on bottom half of toasted rolls. Top with roasted pepper strips. Makes 4 servings.

Per serving: *682 calories, 34 g protein, 80 g carbohydrate, 23 g total fat (6 g saturated), 53 mg cholesterol, 1,214 mg sodium, 556 mg potassium*

Barbecued Pork Sandwiches

1 4½- to 5-pound boneless
  pork shoulder roast
½ teaspoon salt
½ teaspoon black pepper
¼ teaspoon celery seed
⅛ teaspoon onion powder

⅛ teaspoon garlic powder
⅛ teaspoon ground cloves
  Dash ground red pepper
  Easy BBQ Sauce
12 French-style rolls, split and
  toasted

Want to have a pig roast without the pig? Borrow another gas grill so you can cook 2 pork shoulder roasts, and you'll have a feast for 24 guests.

1 Trim fat from meat. For rub, in a small mixing bowl combine salt, black pepper, celery seed, onion powder, garlic powder, cloves, and red pepper. Sprinkle rub evenly over meat; rub in with your fingers.

2 Preheat gas grill. Adjust heat for indirect cooking. Place pork roast on a rack in a roasting pan on the grill rack over medium heat. Add ½ inch of water to pan. Cover and grill about 4 hours or till very tender, adding additional water to pan, if necessary. Let pork roast stand, loosely covered with foil, for 30 minutes. Shred pork with 2 forks. Stir meat into Easy BBQ Sauce; heat through. Spoon pork onto toasted rolls. Makes 12 servings.

Easy BBQ Sauce: In a medium saucepan combine one 8-ounce can *tomato sauce*, 1 cup *catsup*, 1 cup chopped *onion*, ½ cup chopped *green pepper*, and 2 tablespoons *brown sugar*. Stir in ¼ cup *vinegar*, 2 tablespoons *Worcestershire sauce*, 1 tablespoon prepared *mustard*, 2 teaspoons *chili powder*, and 1 large clove *garlic*, minced. Bring to boiling. Reduce heat and simmer, covered, for 15 minutes.

Per serving: *724 calories, 43 g protein, 88 g carbohydrate, 22 g total fat (7 g saturated), 112 mg cholesterol, 1,383 mg sodium, 782 mg potassium*

Cajun-Style Chicken Pitas

To prevent your pita bread from cracking when folding it over the chicken, wrap it in plastic wrap and microwave on 100% power (high) for 30 to 45 seconds or till softened.

4 **large boneless, skinless chicken breast halves (1 pound total)**
½ **cup teriyaki sauce**
1 **tablespoon snipped fresh thyme or 1 teaspoon dried thyme, crushed**
½ to ¾ **teaspoon ground white pepper**
½ to ¾ **teaspoon ground black pepper**

¼ **teaspoon garlic powder**
¼ **teaspoon ground red pepper**
¼ **cup mayonnaise or salad dressing**
2 **teaspoons prepared horseradish**
4 **whole wheat pita bread rounds**
2 **cups shredded lettuce**

1 Rinse chicken; pat dry. Place in a plastic bag set in a shallow dish. Pour teriyaki sauce over chicken. Close bag. Marinate in refrigerator for 6 to 24 hours, turning occasionally.

2 Drain chicken, discarding marinade. In a small bowl combine thyme, white pepper, black pepper, garlic powder, and red pepper. Sprinkle pepper mixture evenly over both sides of chicken breasts; rub it in with your fingers.

3 Preheat gas grill. Adjust heat for direct cooking. Place chicken on grill rack over medium heat. Cover and grill for 12 to 15 minutes or till chicken is tender and no longer pink, turning once halfway through. Cut chicken into bite-size strips.

4 Meanwhile, combine mayonnaise or salad dressing and horseradish. Spread about 1 tablespoon of the mayonnaise mixture over each pita round; top with lettuce. Divide chicken strips among pitas. Fold 2 sides over chicken; secure with a wooden toothpick. Makes 4 servings.

Indirect Grilling: Preheat gas grill. Adjust heat for indirect cooking. Place chicken on grill rack over medium heat. Cover and grill for 15 to 18 minutes or till chicken is tender and no longer pink. Continue as directed above.

Per serving: 334 calories, 27 g protein, 24 g carbohydrate, 15 g total fat (3 g saturated), 67 mg cholesterol, 627 mg sodium, 383 mg potassium

Grilled Turkey Sandwiches Monterey

4 turkey breast tenderloin steaks (1 pound total)
2 teaspoons lemon-pepper seasoning
4 slices Monterey Jack cheese
8 ½-inch-thick slices French bread, toasted

2 tablespoons buttermilk ranch salad dressing or Green Goddess salad dressing
4 tomato slices
1 small avocado, seeded, peeled, and thinly sliced

Tomato, avocado, and cheese tastefully top these tender and moist turkey sandwiches.

1 Rinse turkey; pat dry. Sprinkle both sides of turkey with lemon-pepper seasoning; rub in with your fingers.

2 Preheat gas grill. Adjust heat for direct cooking. Place turkey on grill rack over medium heat. Cover and grill for 12 to 15 minutes or till turkey is tender and no longer pink, turning once halfway through. Top each turkey steak with a cheese slice for the last 2 minutes of grilling.

3 Serve on French bread. Top with salad dressing, tomato slices, and avocado slices. Makes 4 servings.

Indirect Grilling: Preheat gas grill. Adjust heat for indirect cooking. Place turkey on a grill rack over medium heat. Cover and grill for 15 to 18 minutes or till turkey is tender and no longer pink. Continue as directed above.

Per serving: 475 calories, 32 g protein, 38 g carbohydrate, 22 g total fat (7 g saturated), 73 mg cholesterol, 1,174 mg sodium, 517 mg potassium

Cheddar-Chicken Sandwiches

4 large boneless, skinless
   chicken breast halves
   (1 pound total)
⅓ cup lemon juice
2 tablespoons olive oil or
   cooking oil
1 tablespoon snipped fresh
   basil or 1 teaspoon dried
   basil, crushed
2 teaspoons snipped fresh
   parsley

1 teaspoon prepared
   horseradish
4 slices cheddar cheese
4 individual French-style rolls
   or hamburger buns, split
   and toasted
4 slices crisp-cooked bacon,
   halved crosswise
4 tomato slices

1 Rinse chicken; pat dry. Place in a plastic bag set in a shallow dish.
For marinade, combine lemon juice, oil, basil, parsley, and horseradish.
Pour over chicken. Close bag. Marinate in refrigerator for 4 to 24
hours, turning occasionally.

2 Drain chicken, reserving marinade. Preheat gas grill. Adjust heat for
direct cooking. Place chicken on grill rack over medium heat. Cover and
grill for 12 to 15 minutes or till chicken is tender and no longer pink,
turning once and brushing with marinade halfway through. Top each
chicken breast with a cheese slice for the last 2 minutes of grilling.
Discard any remaining marinade.

3 Serve on French-style rolls. Top with bacon and tomato slices. Makes
4 servings.

Indirect Grilling: Preheat gas grill. Adjust heat for indirect cooking.
Place chicken on a grill rack over medium heat. Cover and grill for 15 to
18 minutes or till tender and no longer pink, turning once and brushing
with remaining marinade halfway through. Continue as directed above.

*Per serving: 1,040 calories, 64 g protein, 79 g carbohydrate, 51 g total fat
(27 g saturated), 184 mg cholesterol, 1,622 mg sodium, 520 mg potassium*

Orange-Teriyaki Chicken Sandwiches

4 large boneless, skinless
  chicken breast halves
  (1 pound total)
⅓ cup teriyaki sauce
⅓ cup frozen orange juice
  concentrate, thawed

½ teaspoon toasted sesame oil
⅛ teaspoon garlic powder
4 kaiser rolls or whole wheat
  buns, split and toasted
1 small orange, peeled and cut
  crosswise into 4 slices

An Oriental-style marinade flavors these tasty chicken breast sandwiches.

1 Rinse chicken; pat dry. Place in a plastic bag set in a shallow dish. For marinade, combine teriyaki sauce, orange juice concentrate, sesame oil, and garlic powder. Pour over chicken. Close bag. Marinate in refrigerator for 6 to 24 hours, turning occasionally.

2 Drain chicken, reserving marinade. Preheat gas grill. Adjust heat for direct cooking. Place chicken on grill rack over medium heat. Cover and grill for 12 to 15 minutes or till chicken is tender and no longer pink, turning once and brushing with marinade halfway through. Discard any remaining marinade.

3 Serve on kaiser rolls. Top with orange slices. Makes 4 servings.

Indirect Grilling: Preheat gas grill. Adjust heat for indirect cooking. Place chicken on a grill rack over medium heat. Cover and grill for 15 to 18 minutes or till tender and no longer pink, turning once and brushing with remaining marinade halfway through. Continue as directed above.

Per serving: 314 calories, 28 g protein, 38 g carbohydrate, 5 g total fat (1 g saturated), 59 mg cholesterol, 822 mg sodium, 354 mg potassium

Soak It with Sauce

With the single stroke of a basting brush, you can make that chicken sweet-and-sour or those ribs hot-and-spicy. The versatile sauces in this chapter can help you do that. From slightly sweet to fiery hot to super fast, these snappy sauces give your grill favorites new life.

In This Chapter:

Spicy 'N' Sweet Ribs

1 tablespoon brown sugar
½ teaspoon onion powder
¼ teaspoon salt
¼ teaspoon dry mustard
¼ teaspoon ground turmeric
⅛ to ¼ teaspoon ground red pepper

4 pounds pork loin back ribs or meaty pork spareribs, cut into serving-size pieces
½ cup apple juice
¼ cup hoisin sauce
2 tablespoons dry sherry or apple juice
2 to 3 teaspoons grated gingerroot

Keep a good supply of big, thick napkins handy when you serve these zesty ribs.

1 In a small mixing bowl combine brown sugar, onion powder, salt, dry mustard, turmeric, and red pepper; rub spice mixture over ribs. Cover and refrigerate ribs for 2 to 3 hours.

2 Meanwhile, for sauce, in a saucepan combine apple juice, hoisin sauce, sherry or apple juice, and gingerroot; bring to boiling. Remove from heat; set aside.

3 Preheat gas grill. Adjust heat for indirect cooking. Place ribs on grill rack over medium heat. Cover and grill for 1¼ to 1½ hours or till ribs are tender and no longer pink. Brush generously with sauce the last 15 minutes of grilling. Makes 6 servings.

Per serving: 434 calories, 30 g protein, 5 g carbohydrate, 31 g total fat (12 g saturated), 124 mg cholesterol, 492 mg sodium, 380 mg potassium

Baby Back Ribs with Mustard Sauce

Just before serving, slather these showstopping ribs with leftover sauce.

⅓ cup packed brown sugar
¼ cup finely chopped onion
¼ cup vinegar
¼ cup prepared mustard

½ teaspoon celery seed
¼ teaspoon garlic powder
4 pounds pork loin back ribs or meaty pork spareribs, cut into serving-size pieces

1 For sauce, in a saucepan combine brown sugar, onion, vinegar, mustard, celery seed, and garlic powder. Bring to boiling, stirring till sugar dissolves.

2 Preheat gas grill. Adjust heat for indirect cooking. Place ribs on grill rack over medium heat. Cover and grill for 1¼ to 1½ hours or till ribs are tender and no pink remains. Brush occasionally with sauce the last 15 minutes of grilling. Makes 6 servings.

Per serving: 572 calories, 38 g protein, 11 g carbohydrate, 40 g total fat (15 g saturated), 158 mg cholesterol, 256 mg sodium, 491 mg potassium

Country-Style Ribs with Apple Sauce

1 cup apple butter
2 tablespoons vinegar
1 teaspoon horseradish mustard
½ teaspoon celery seed

¼ teaspoon sugar
¼ teaspoon salt
¼ teaspoon garlic powder
⅛ teaspoon pepper
2½ to 3 pounds pork country-style ribs

1 For sauce, in a pan mix apple butter, vinegar, mustard, celery seed, sugar, salt, garlic powder, and pepper. Bring just to boiling; stir often.

2 Trim fat from meat. Preheat gas grill. Adjust heat for indirect cooking. Place ribs on grill rack over medium heat. Cover; grill for 1½ to 2 hours or till tender and no pink remains. Brush occasionally with sauce the last 15 minutes of grilling. Heat remaining sauce; pass with ribs. Serves 4.

Per serving: 541 calories, 33 g protein, 38 g carbohydrate, 29 g total fat (10 g saturated), 129 mg cholesterol, 245 mg sodium, 746 mg potassium

Extra-Hot 'N' Spicy Barbecued Ribs

3 to 4 pounds beef chuck short ribs with bone or 2 to 2½ pounds without bone
⅓ cup chopped onion
1 clove garlic, minced
1 tablespoon cooking oil
1½ cups catsup

⅓ cup vinegar
¼ cup molasses
1 teaspoon ground red pepper
1 teaspoon chili powder
1 to 2 teaspoons bottled hot pepper sauce
½ teaspoon dry mustard

These beef ribs, dripping with sauce, are truly finger-lickin' good.

1 Trim fat from meat. Cut ribs into serving-size pieces. Place ribs in a Dutch oven; add enough water to cover ribs. Bring to boiling. Reduce heat and simmer, covered, about 1½ hours or till meat is tender. Drain ribs.

2 Meanwhile, for sauce, in a medium saucepan cook onion and garlic in hot oil till onion is tender but not brown. Stir in catsup, vinegar, molasses, red pepper, chili powder, hot pepper sauce, and dry mustard. Bring to boiling. Reduce heat and simmer, uncovered, for 15 minutes, stirring occasionally.

3 Preheat gas grill. Adjust heat for indirect cooking. Place precooked ribs on grill rack over medium heat. Brush with sauce. Cover and grill for 15 minutes, turning once halfway through and brushing frequently with sauce. Pass any remaining sauce. Makes 6 servings.

Per serving: *429 calories, 43 g protein, 30 g carbohydrate, 15 g total fat (5 g saturated), 129 mg cholesterol, 904 mg sodium, 865 mg potassium*

T-Bones with Mushroom-Wine Sauce

Dress up a grilled steak with this simple, but full-flavored sauce.

2 1-pound beef T-bone or porterhouse steaks, cut 1 inch thick
1 cup sliced fresh shiitake mushrooms or other mushrooms
⅓ cup chopped onion
1 clove garlic, minced

2 tablespoons margarine or butter
1 tablespoon cornstarch
⅔ cup water
⅓ cup dry red wine
½ teaspoon instant beef bouillon granules
1 tablespoon snipped fresh parsley

1 Trim fat from meat. Preheat gas grill. Adjust heat for direct cooking. Place steaks on grill rack over medium heat. Cover and grill for 16 to 20 minutes for rare (140°) or 20 to 24 minutes for medium (160°).

2 Meanwhile, for sauce, in a medium saucepan cook mushrooms, onion, and garlic in margarine or butter for 4 to 5 minutes or till tender. Stir in cornstarch; add water, red wine, and bouillon granules. Cook and stir till thickened and bubbly. Cook and stir for 2 minutes more. Stir in parsley.

3 To serve, cut steaks into serving-size pieces. Pass sauce with steaks. Makes 4 servings.

Indirect Grilling: Preheat gas grill. Adjust heat for indirect cooking. Place steaks on grill rack over medium heat. Cover and grill for 16 to 20 minutes for rare (140°) or 22 to 26 minutes for medium (160°). Continue as directed above.

Per serving: 394 calories, 39 g protein, 7 g carbohydrate, 21 g total fat (7 g saturated), 113 mg cholesterol, 196 mg sodium, 605 mg potassium

Rib-Eyes with Blackberry Sauce

2 beef rib-eye steaks, cut
   1 inch thick (about
   1½ pounds total)
¼ cup blackberry jam
2 tablespoons red wine vinegar

½ teaspoon Worcestershire
   sauce
⅛ teaspoon pepper
½ cup fresh or frozen
   blackberries, thawed

1 Cut steaks into 4 equal portions. Preheat gas grill. Adjust heat for direct cooking. Place steaks on grill rack over medium heat. Cover and grill for 16 to 20 minutes for rare (140°) or 20 to 24 minutes for medium (160°).

2 Meanwhile, for sauce, in a small saucepan cook jam, vinegar, Worcestershire sauce, and pepper, stirring till jam melts. Pour sauce over steaks; top with blackberries. Makes 4 servings.

Indirect Grilling: Preheat gas grill. Adjust heat for indirect cooking. Place steaks on grill rack over medium heat. Cover and grill for 16 to 20 minutes for rare (140°) or 22 to 26 minutes for medium (160°).

Per serving: 365 calories, 34 g protein, 17 g carbohydrate, 17 g total fat (7 g saturated), 100 mg cholesterol, 100 mg sodium, 518 mg potassium

Filet Mignon with Peppercorn Sauce

1 teaspoon cracked whole
black peppercorns

2 10-ounce beef tenderloin
steaks, cut 1 inch thick
Peppercorn-Mustard Sauce

1 Sprinkle cracked black pepper over both sides of steaks, pressing pepper into steaks. Preheat gas grill. Adjust heat for direct cooking. Place steaks on grill rack over medium heat. Cover and grill for 16 to 20 minutes for rare (140°) or 20 to 22 minutes for medium (160°). Serve steaks with Peppercorn-Mustard Sauce. Makes 2 servings.

Indirect Grilling: Preheat gas grill. Adjust heat for indirect cooking. Place steaks on grill rack over medium heat. Cover and grill for 16 to 20 minutes for rare (140°) or 20 to 22 minutes for medium (160°).

Peppercorn-Mustard Sauce: Mash 1 to 2 teaspoons drained *pickled whole green peppercorns;* set aside. In a small saucepan melt 2 teaspoons *margarine or butter.* Stir in ½ teaspoon *all-purpose flour,* dash *salt,* and dash *pepper.* Stir in ½ cup *half-and-half or light cream* all at once. Cook and stir over medium heat till thickened and bubbly. Cook and stir 1 minute more. Stir in 1 tablespoon *Dijon-style mustard* and the mashed peppercorns. Heat through.

Per serving: 510 calories, 56 g protein, 5 g carbohydrate, 28 g total fat (11 g saturated), 179 mg cholesterol, 443 mg sodium, 919 mg potassium

Saucy Cherry Chicken Pieces

1 cup cherry preserves
1 tablespoon margarine or
   butter
½ teaspoon finely shredded
   lemon peel
2 tablespoons lemon juice

½ teaspoon ground cinnamon
¼ teaspoon ground allspice
⅛ teaspoon salt
   Dash ground cloves
2 to 2½ pounds meaty chicken
   pieces (breasts, thighs,
   and drumsticks)

Some lemon and spices stirred into a jar of cherry preserves makes this quick-and-tasty sauce.

1 For sauce, in a small saucepan combine cherry preserves, margarine or butter, lemon peel, lemon juice, cinnamon, allspice, salt, and cloves. Cook and stir till combined.

2 Remove skin from chicken, if desired. Rinse chicken; pat dry. Preheat gas grill. Adjust heat for direct cooking. Place chicken, bone side up, on grill rack over medium heat. Cover and grill for 35 to 45 minutes or till tender and no longer pink, turning once halfway through. Brush with sauce frequently the last 10 minutes of grilling. Makes 4 servings.

Indirect Grilling: Preheat gas grill. Adjust heat for indirect cooking. Place chicken, bone side down, on grill rack over medium heat. Cover and grill for 50 to 60 minutes or till tender and no longer pink, turning once halfway through. Brush with sauce frequently the last 10 minutes of grilling.

Per serving: *519 calories, 33 g protein, 61 g carbohydrate, 16 g total fat (4 g saturated), 104 mg cholesterol, 200 mg sodium, 339 mg potassium*

Saucy Caribbean Chicken

If your taste buds want a hotter sauce, don't seed the jalapeño pepper.

¼ cup chili sauce
2 green onions, thinly sliced
1 jalapeño pepper, seeded and chopped
1 clove garlic, halved
1 tablespoon cooking oil
1 tablespoon lemon juice

1 tablespoon chicken broth or water
¼ teaspoon salt
¼ teaspoon ground ginger
¼ teaspoon ground allspice
2 to 2½ pounds meaty chicken pieces (breasts, thighs, and drumsticks)

1 For sauce, in a small mixing bowl combine chili sauce, green onions, jalapeño pepper, garlic, oil, lemon juice, chicken broth or water, salt, ginger, and allspice.

2 Remove skin from chicken, if desired. Rinse chicken; pat dry. Preheat gas grill. Adjust heat for direct cooking. Place chicken, bone side up, on grill rack over medium heat. Cover and grill for 35 to 45 minutes or till tender and no longer pink, turning once halfway through. Brush with sauce frequently the last 10 minutes of grilling. Makes 4 servings.

Indirect Grilling: Preheat gas grill. Adjust heat for indirect cooking. Place chicken, bone side down, on grill rack over medium heat. Cover and grill for 50 to 60 minutes or till tender and no longer pink, turning once halfway through. Brush with sauce frequently the last 10 minutes of grilling.

Per serving: *308 calories, 34 g protein, 5 g carbohydrate, 16 g total fat (4 g saturated), 104 mg cholesterol, 439 mg sodium, 339 mg potassium*

Turkey Thighs with Apricot Sauce

3 tablespoons brown sugar
1 tablespoon cornstarch
1¼ cups apricot nectar
2 tablespoons catsup

1 tablespoon horseradish
   mustard or prepared
   mustard
1 teaspoon finely shredded
   orange peel
2 small turkey thighs
   (2 pounds total)

1 For sauce, in a medium saucepan combine brown sugar and corn-starch. Stir in apricot nectar, catsup, horseradish mustard, and orange peel. Cook and stir over medium heat till thickened and bubbly. Cook and stir 2 minutes more. Remove from heat; set aside.

2 Remove skin from turkey thighs, if desired. Rinse turkey; pat dry. Insert meat thermometer into center of one of the turkey thighs, not touching bone.

3 Preheat gas grill. Adjust heat for indirect cooking. Place turkey thighs, bone side down, on a rack in a roasting pan over medium heat. Cover and grill for 1¼ to 1¾ hours or till thermometer registers 180° to 185°. Brush frequently with sauce the last 10 minutes of grilling.

4 To serve, cut turkey meat from the bones. Pass remaining sauce. Makes 4 servings.

Per serving: 305 calories, 35 g protein, 26 g carbohydrate, 7 g total fat (2 g saturated), 83 mg cholesterol, 236 mg sodium, 471 mg potassium

Salmon with Pineapple-Cilantro Sauce

When seeding and chopping a fresh jalapeño pepper, protect your hands with plastic gloves so the oils in the pepper don't irritate your skin. Also, avoid direct contact with your eyes. Wash your hands thoroughly when you're finished with the chili pepper.

4 6-ounce fresh or frozen salmon or halibut steaks, cut 1 inch thick
1 8-ounce can crushed pineapple
¼ cup chopped sweet red pepper
1 fresh jalapeño chili pepper, seeded and chopped

1 clove garlic, minced
Lime juice
2 teaspoons cornstarch
Cooking oil
2 tablespoons margarine or butter
1 to 2 tablespoons snipped fresh cilantro

1 Thaw fish, if frozen. For sauce, drain pineapple, reserving juice. In a small saucepan combine pineapple, sweet red pepper, jalapeño pepper, and garlic. Add enough lime juice to reserved pineapple juice to make ½ cup; stir in cornstarch. Add pineapple juice mixture to mixture in saucepan. Cook and stir over medium heat till thickened and bubbly. Cook and stir 2 minutes more. Keep warm.

2 Brush grill rack lightly with oil. Preheat gas grill. Adjust heat for direct cooking. Place fish on grill rack over medium heat. Cover and grill for 8 to 10 minutes or just till fish begins to flake easily, turning once halfway through. Brush occasionally with the melted margarine or butter.

3 Just before serving, stir cilantro into sauce. Serve salmon with sauce. Makes 4 servings.

Indirect Grilling: Brush grill rack lightly with oil. Preheat gas grill. Adjust heat for indirect cooking. Place fish on grill rack over medium heat. Cover and grill for 8 to 12 minutes or just till fish begins to flake easily, turning once halfway through. Brush occasionally with the melted margarine or butter. Continue as directed above.

Per serving: 265 calories, 25 g protein, 12 g carbohydrate, 13 g total fat (2 g saturated), 31 mg cholesterol, 172 mg sodium, 350 mg potassium

Lobster Tails with Chive Butter

**4 medium fresh or frozen
  rock lobster tails
  (about 5 ounces each)**
½ cup margarine or butter

**2 tablespoons snipped fresh
  chives**
**1 teaspoon finely shredded
  lemon peel**

*Complement this
elegant seafood
entrée with a
side dish of rice
pilaf, fresh spinach
salads, and a
glass of dry white
wine.*

1 Thaw lobster, if frozen. Rinse lobster; pat dry. Butterfly tails by using kitchen shears or a sharp knife to cut lengthwise through centers of hard top shells and meat. Cut to, but not through, bottoms of shells. Press shell halves of tails apart with your fingers.

2 For sauce, in a small saucepan melt margarine or butter. Stir in chives and lemon peel.

3 Preheat gas grill. Adjust heat for direct cooking. Brush lobster meat with sauce. Place lobster tails, meat side down, on grill rack over medium heat. Cover and grill 4 minutes. Turn meat side up. Brush with sauce and continue grilling for 3 to 5 minutes more or till lobster meat turns opaque.

4 Heat remaining sauce, stirring occasionally. Serve sauce in small cups for dipping. Makes 4 servings.

Indirect Grilling: Preheat gas grill. Adjust heat for indirect cooking. Brush lobster meat with sauce. Place lobster tails, meat side down, on grill rack over medium heat. Cover and grill for 6 minutes. Turn meat side up. Brush with sauce and continue grilling for 6 to 8 minutes more or till lobster meat turns opaque. Continue as directed above.

Per serving: 293 calories, 19 g protein, 2 g carbohydrate, 23 g total fat (4 g saturated), 65 mg cholesterol, 612 mg sodium, 335 mg potassium

Top It with Salsa

Salsas aren't just for chips anymore! These tongue-tingling toppers, made with only the freshest ingredients, are a powerhouse of flavor. They can add a sweetness, a crunch, or a burning fire to grilled poultry, fish, and meat.

In This Chapter:

Spiced Chops with Melon Salsa

¼ teaspoon garlic salt
¼ teaspoon ground ginger
¼ teaspoon dry mustard
¼ teaspoon pepper

4 pork loin or rib chops, cut
   1¼ inches thick
   (about 2¼ pounds total)
Melon Salsa

1 For rub mixture, in a small mixing bowl combine garlic salt, ginger, dry mustard, and pepper. Trim fat from meat. Rub both sides of pork chops with rub mixture.

2 Preheat gas grill. Adjust heat for direct cooking. Place chops on grill rack over medium heat. Cover and grill for 25 to 35 minutes or till juices run clear, turning once halfway through. Serve chops with Melon Salsa. Makes 4 servings.

Indirect Grilling: Preheat gas grill. Adjust heat for indirect cooking. Place chops on grill rack over medium heat. Cover and grill for 35 to 45 minutes or till juices run clear, turning once halfway through. Continue as directed above.

Melon Salsa: In a medium mixing bowl combine ⅓ cup seeded, finely chopped *watermelon*, ⅓ cup finely chopped *honeydew melon*, ⅓ cup finely chopped *cantaloupe*, ¼ cup finely chopped *jicama*, 2 tablespoons thinly sliced *green onion*, 2 tablespoons snipped fresh *cilantro*, 2 tablespoons *lime juice*, and 1 *jalapeño pepper*, seeded and chopped. Cover and refrigerate for 4 to 6 hours. Makes about 1½ cups.

Per serving: *334 calories, 37 g protein, 7 g carbohydrate, 17 g total fat (6 g saturated), 115 mg cholesterol, 220 mg sodium, 644 mg potassium*

You can usually buy small amounts of melon in the deli or produce section of your supermarket.

Turkey with Mediterranean-Style Salsa

This tempting topping is fresh tasting and full of crunch.

4 **turkey breast tenderloin steaks (1 pound total)**
¼ **cup mayonnaise or salad dressing**
¼ **cup clear Italian salad dressing**
   Dash ground red pepper
⅔ **cup chopped, seeded tomato**
½ **cup chopped, seeded cucumber**
⅓ **cup chopped pitted ripe olives**

3 **tablespoons finely chopped onion**
2 **tablespoons clear Italian salad dressing**
1 **tablespoon snipped fresh basil or 1 teaspoon dried basil, crushed**
½ **teaspoon sugar**
⅛ **teaspoon pepper**
¼ **cup crumbled feta cheese**

1 Rinse turkey; pat dry. Place in a plastic bag set in a shallow dish. For marinade, combine mayonnaise or salad dressing, the ¼ cup Italian salad dressing, and red pepper; pour over turkey. Close bag. Marinate in refrigerator for 6 to 24 hours, turning occasionally.

2 For salsa, in a medium mixing bowl combine tomato, cucumber, olives, onion, the 2 tablespoons Italian salad dressing, basil, sugar, and pepper. Cover and chill for 6 to 24 hours.

3 Drain turkey, reserving marinade. Preheat gas grill. Adjust heat for direct cooking. Place turkey on grill rack over medium heat. Cover and grill for 12 to 15 minutes or till turkey is tender and no longer pink, brushing occasionally with reserved marinade.

4 Just before serving, stir feta cheese into salsa. Spoon salsa over turkey. Makes 4 servings.

Indirect Grilling: Preheat gas grill. Adjust heat for indirect cooking. Place turkey on grill rack over medium heat. Cover and grill about 20 minutes or till turkey is tender and no longer pink, brushing occasionally with reserved marinade. Continue as directed above.

Per serving: *362 calories, 23 g protein, 7 g carbohydrate, 27 g total fat (5 g saturated), 64 mg cholesterol, 433 mg sodium, 358 mg potassium*

Chicken with Tropical Fruit Salsa

4 large boneless, skinless
  chicken breast halves
  (1 pound total)
⅓ cup pineapple juice
  concentrate, thawed
2 tablespoons soy sauce
2 tablespoons cooking oil
1 teaspoon grated gingerroot
¼ teaspoon dry mustard
⅛ teaspoon pepper
1 clove garlic, minced
1 small papaya, peeled,
  seeded, and chopped
  (1⅓ cups)

2 kiwi fruit, peeled and
  chopped (1 cup)
2 tablespoons finely chopped
  onion
1 to 2 jalapeño peppers,
  seeded and chopped
  (1 to 2 tablespoons)
1 tablespoon snipped fresh
  cilantro, parsley, or mint
  Several dashes bottled hot
  pepper sauce
3 tablespoons water
1 tablespoon pineapple juice
  concentrate, thawed

Guests will give you rave reviews for this exciting, colorful, lowfat entrée.

1 Rinse chicken; pat dry. Place chicken in a plastic bag set in a shallow dish. For marinade, combine the ⅓ cup pineapple juice concentrate, soy sauce, oil, gingerroot, dry mustard, pepper, and garlic; pour over chicken. Close bag. Marinate in refrigerator 6 to 24 hours; turn occasionally.

2 Meanwhile, for salsa, in a mixing bowl combine papaya; kiwi fruit; onion; jalapeño pepper; cilantro, parsley, or mint; and hot pepper sauce. Place about 1 cup of the fruit mixture in a blender container or food processor bowl with water and the 1 tablespoon pineapple juice concentrate. Cover and blend or process just till smooth. Stir into remaining fruit mixture. Cover and chill for several hours or overnight, stirring occasionally.

3 Drain chicken, reserving marinade. Preheat gas grill. Adjust heat for direct cooking. Place chicken on grill rack over medium heat. Cover and grill for 12 to 15 minutes or till tender and no longer pink, turning once halfway through and brushing occasionally with reserved marinade.

4 Serve chicken breast halves with fruit salsa. Makes 4 serving.

Per serving: *233 calories, 23g protein, 19 g carbohydrate, 7 g total fat (1 g saturated), 59 mg cholesterol, 287mg sodium, 542 mg potassium*

Swordfish with Berry Salsa

When fresh blueberries aren't available, make this surprising and unusual salsa with chopped pears.

4 **5- to 6-ounce fresh or frozen swordfish, shark, or halibut steaks, cut 1 inch thick**

½ **cup chopped fresh strawberries**

¼ **cup fresh blueberries**

1 **tablespoon snipped fresh cilantro**

1 **tablespoon finely chopped onion**

1 **teaspoon orange juice concentrate, thawed**

1 **jalapeño pepper, seeded and chopped**

2 **tablespoons orange juice concentrate, thawed**

1 Thaw fish, if frozen. For salsa, in a small mixing bowl combine strawberries, blueberries, cilantro, onion, the 1 teaspoon orange juice concentrate, and jalapeño pepper. Set aside.

2 Brush both sides of fish steaks with the 2 tablespoons orange juice concentrate. Brush grill rack lightly with oil. Preheat gas grill. Adjust heat for direct cooking. Place fish steaks on rack over medium heat. Cover and grill for 8 to 12 minutes or just till fish begins to flake easily, turning once. Serve fish with salsa. Makes 4 servings.

Per serving: 202 calories, 29 g protein, 7 g carbohydrate, 6 g total fat (2 g saturated), 56 mg cholesterol, 129 mg sodium, 539 mg potassium

Fish with Black Bean-Corn Salsa

**6 4-ounce fresh or frozen red
  snapper or whitefish fillets,
  cut ½ to ¾ inch thick**
**2 tablespoons olive oil or
  cooking oil**

1 tablespoon lime juice
⅛ teaspoon garlic powder
  Black Bean-Corn Salsa

1 Thaw fish, if frozen. In a small mixing bowl combine oil, lime juice, and garlic powder; brush over both sides of fish fillets.

2 Place fish in a greased grill basket (or on a large, greased piece of heavy foil with slits cut in it). Preheat gas grill. Adjust heat for direct cooking. Place grill basket (or foil) on grill rack over medium heat. Cover and grill for 6 to 8 minutes or just till fish begins to flake easily, turning basket (or fish) after 4 minutes. Serve with Black Bean-Corn Salsa. Makes 6 servings.

Indirect Grilling: Preheat gas grill. Adjust heat for indirect cooking. Place fish on a large, greased piece of heavy foil with slits cut in it. Place foil with fish on a grill rack over medium heat. Cover and grill for 4 to 9 minutes or just till fish begins to flake easily. Continue as directed above.

Black Bean-Corn Salsa: In a medium mixing bowl combine 1½ cups chopped, seeded *tomato* (2 large tomatoes); ½ of a 15-ounce can (¾ cup) *black beans*, rinsed and drained; ½ cup frozen *whole kernel corn*, thawed; 3 tablespoons thinly sliced *green onion*; 2 tablespoons snipped fresh *cilantro*; 2 tablespoons *olive oil* or *cooking oil*; 1 tablespoon *lime juice*; ¼ teaspoon *salt*; ¼ teaspoon ground *cumin*; ⅛ teaspoon *pepper*; and 1 *jalapeño pepper*, chopped (not seeded). Cover and refrigerate for 6 to 24 hours.

Per serving: *239 calories, 26 g protein, 10 g carbohydrate, 11 g total fat (2 g saturated), 42 mg cholesterol, 231 mg sodium, 666 mg potassium*

If you have any of this colorful salsa leftover, you can store it in the refrigerator for 3 to 5 days. It's great on grilled steaks or chops, too.

Gloss It with Glaze

A glaze is a thin type of sauce that usually stays glossy, even after cooking. The glazes in this chapter take on lots of distinctive flavors–mustard, chutney, even cranberry–and are brushed on all your favorite meats and poultry cuts.

In This Chapter:

Easy Pineapple-Glazed Ham Steak

1½- to 2-pound fully cooked
    center-cut ham slice, cut
    1 inch thick
1 tablespoon margarine or
    butter

¼ cup pineapple, apricot, or
    apricot-pineapple preserves
    or all-fruit spread
1 tablespoon Dijon-style
    mustard or horseradish
    mustard
    Dash ground cloves

When grilled over direct heat, this tasty ham steak is ready to eat in just about 20 minutes.

1 Trim fat from ham. Slash edges of ham at 1-inch intervals. For glaze, in a small saucepan melt margarine or butter. Stir in preserves or all-fruit spread, mustard, and cloves. Heat through.

2 Preheat gas grill. Adjust heat for direct cooking. Place ham steak on grill rack over medium-high heat. Cover and grill for 10 minutes. Turn ham and brush with glaze. Grill for 6 to 8 minutes more or till heated through. Makes 6 servings.

Indirect Grilling: Preheat gas grill. Adjust heat for indirect cooking. Place ham steak on grill rack over medium-high heat. Cover and grill for 15 minutes. Turn ham and brush with glaze. Grill for 5 to 9 minutes more or till heated through.

Per serving: 235 calories, 29 g protein, 10 g carbohydrate, 8 g total fat (2 g saturated), 62 mg cholesterol, 1,591 mg sodium, 375 g potassium

Honey-Mustard Pork Chops

Mustard, sweetened with honey and a touch of orange juice gives a tangy flavor to this glaze. Try it on chicken, too.

¼ cup honey
2 tablespoons Dijon-style
   mustard
1 tablespoon orange juice
½ teaspoon white wine
   Worcestershire sauce

⅛ teaspoon onion powder
4 boneless pork loin chops,
   cut 1¼ inches thick
   (1 to 1½ pounds)

1 For glaze, in a small saucepan combine honey, mustard, orange juice, Worcestershire sauce, and onion powder. Boil gently about 2 minutes or till sauce is slightly thickened.

Indirect Grilling: Preheat gas grill. Adjust heat for indirect cooking. Place chops on grill rack over medium heat. Cover and grill for 35 to 50 minutes or till juices run clear, turning once halfway through and brushing with glaze often. Makes 4 servings.

Per serving: 212 calories, 17 g protein, 18 g carbohydrate, 8 g total fat (3 g saturated), 51 mg cholesterol, 234 mg sodium, 236 mg potassium

Pork Roast with Plum Glaze

½ cup plum preserves
2 tablespoons soy sauce
1 tablespoon snipped fresh
  sage or ½ teaspoon dried
  sage, crushed

1 tablespoon lemon juice
1 tablespoon cooking oil
1 2-pound boneless pork top
  loin roast (single loin)

You can also use this easy, sage-scented glaze on pork chops.

1 For glaze, in a small saucepan combine plum preserves, soy sauce, sage, lemon juice, and cooking oil. Heat till preserves melt, stirring occasionally.

2 Trim fat from meat. Insert a meat thermometer near center of roast.

Indirect Grilling: Preheat gas grill. Adjust heat for indirect cooking. Place pork roast on a rack in a roasting pan on the grill rack over medium-low heat. Cover and grill for 1 to 1¼ hours or till meat thermometer registers 160° to 170°, brushing occasionally with glaze after 30 minutes. Slice to serve. Pass any remaining glaze. Makes 8 servings.

Per serving: *208 calories, 16 g protein, 15 g carbohydrate, 9 g total fat (3 g saturated), 51 mg cholesterol, 298 mg sodium, 232 mg potassium*

Currant-Glazed Chops

These thick pork chops are wrapped with partially cooked bacon, then brushed with a shiny glaze.

4 slices bacon
4 boneless pork loin chops, cut 1½ inch thick (1 to 1½ pounds)
½ cup currant jelly

1 tablespoon snipped fresh chives
1 tablespoon coarse-grain brown mustard
½ teaspoon lemon-pepper seasoning

1 In a skillet cook bacon till nearly done but not crisp. Wrap one bacon slice around each chop. Secure bacon to chops with wooden toothpicks.

2 For glaze, in a small saucepan combine jelly, chives, brown mustard, and lemon-pepper. Cook and stir just till boiling. Keep warm.

Indirect Grilling: Preheat gas grill. Adjust heat for indirect cooking. Place chops on grill rack over medium heat. Cover and grill for 35 to 50 minutes or till juices run clear, turning once halfway through and brushing with glaze often. Makes 4 servings.

Per serving: 278 calories, 18 g protein, 27 g carbohydrate, 11 g total fat (4 g saturated), 56 mg cholesterol, 333 mg sodium, 271 mg potassium

Mint-Glazed Lamb Chops

¼ cup mint jelly
1 tablespoon dry white wine or
    orange juice
½ teaspoon finely shredded
    orange peel

⅛ teaspoon pepper
8 lamb rib or loin chops or
    4 leg sirloin chops, cut
    1 inch thick (about
    2½ pounds total)

Serve this attention-getting main dish with cooked baby carrots and some crusty Italian bread.

1 For glaze, in a small saucepan combine mint jelly, wine or orange juice, orange peel, and pepper. Heat till smooth.

2 Trim fat from meat. Preheat gas grill. Adjust heat for direct cooking. Place lamb chops on grill rack over medium heat. Cover and grill for 10 to 16 minutes or till desired doneness, turning once halfway through and brushing with glaze often. Makes 4 servings.

Indirect Grilling: Preheat gas grill. Adjust heat for indirect cooking. Place lamb chops on grill rack over medium heat. Cover and grill for 16 to 20 minutes or till desired doneness, turning once halfway through and brushing with glaze often.

Per serving: *254 calories, 26 g protein, 13 g carbohydrate, 10 g total fat (4 g saturated), 86 mg cholesterol, 69 mg sodium, 283 mg potassium*

Chutney-Glazed Lamb Chops

¼ cup chutney
¼ cup unsweetened pineapple
  juice
2 teaspoons Dijon-style
  mustard
1 teaspoon soy sauce

Dash crushed red pepper
1 clove garlic, minced
8 lamb rib or loin chops or
  4 leg sirloin chops, cut
  1 inch thick (about
  2½ pounds total)

1 For glaze, in a blender container or food processor bowl combine chutney, pineapple juice, mustard, soy sauce, red pepper, and garlic. Cover and blend or process till pureed.

2 Trim fat from meat. Preheat gas grill. Adjust heat for direct cooking. Place lamb chops on grill rack over medium heat. Cover and grill 10 to 16 minutes or till desired doneness, turning once halfway through and brushing with glaze often. Makes 4 servings.

Indirect Grilling: Preheat gas grill. Adjust heat for indirect cooking. Place lamb chops on grill rack over medium heat. Cover and grill for 16 to 20 minutes or till desired doneness, turning once halfway through and brushing with glaze often.

Per serving: 321 calories, 32 g protein, 13 g carbohydrate, 15 g total fat (5 g saturated), 104 mg cholesterol, 250 mg sodium, 403 mg potassium

Apricot and Curry Turkey Breast

½ cup apricot preserves
2 tablespoons lemon juice
½ teaspoon curry powder

1 2- to 2½-pound turkey breast half
1 tablespoon cooking oil

Only three ingredients make up this deliciously different glaze.

1 For glaze, in a small saucepan combine apricot preserves, lemon juice, and curry powder. Cook and stir over medium heat till boiling. Cook and stir 1 minute more. Set glaze aside.

2 Remove bone from turkey breast. Rinse turkey; pat dry. Brush turkey with oil. Insert a meat thermometer into the center of turkey breast.

3 Preheat gas grill. Adjust heat for indirect cooking. Place turkey breast on a rack in a roasting pan on the grill rack over medium heat. Cover and grill for 1½ to 2 hours or till thermometer registers 170°. Brush with half of the glaze several times during the last 15 minutes of grilling.

4 Heat remaining glaze and pass with sliced turkey. Makes 6 servings.

Per serving: 318 calories, 34 g protein, 19 g carbohydrate, 11 g total fat (3 g saturated), 88 mg cholesterol, 77 mg sodium, 373 mg potassium

Glazed Sweet 'N' Sour Chicken

Make a complete summertime meal by adding fresh green beans, a crisp lettuce salad, and big glasses of iced tea.

1 tablespoon cornstarch
¼ cup packed brown sugar
⅓ cup chicken broth
¼ cup red wine vinegar
1 tablespoon lemon juice

1 tablespoon catsup
1½ teaspoons soy sauce
¼ teaspoon ground ginger
1 2½- to 3-pound broiler-fryer chicken, cut up

1 For sauce, in a small saucepan combine cornstarch and brown sugar. Stir in the chicken broth, vinegar, lemon juice, catsup, soy sauce, and ginger. Cook and stir till thickened and bubbly. Cook and stir for 2 minutes more.

2 Remove skin from chicken, if desired. Rinse chicken; pat dry. Preheat gas grill. Adjust heat for direct cooking. Place chicken, bone side up, on grill rack over medium heat. Cover and grill for 35 to 45 minutes or till chicken is tender and no longer pink, turning once halfway through. Brush frequently with sauce the last 10 minutes. Makes 4 servings.

Indirect Grilling: Preheat gas grill. Adjust heat for indirect cooking. Place chicken, bone side down, on grill rack over medium heat. Cover and grill for 50 to 60 minutes or till chicken is tender and no longer pink, turning once halfway through. Brush frequently with sauce the last 10 minutes.

Per serving: 337 calories, 31 g protein, 18 g carbohydrate, 15 g total fat (4 g saturated), 99 mg cholesterol, 325 mg sodium, 361 mg potassium

Lime and Red Pepper Grilled Chicken

**2 to 2½ pounds meaty chicken
  pieces (breasts, thighs,
  and drumsticks)**
**1 teaspoon finely shredded
  lime peel**

¼ cup lime juice
2 tablespoons cooking oil
2 cloves garlic, minced
¼ teaspoon onion salt
¼ teaspoon crushed red pepper

This southwestern-style glaze will get your taste buds tingling.

1 Remove skin from chicken, if desired. Rinse chicken; pat dry. For glaze, in a small mixing bowl combine lime peel, lime juice, oil, garlic, onion salt, and red pepper.

2 Preheat gas grill. Adjust the heat for direct cooking. Place chicken, bone side up, on grill rack over medium heat. Cover and grill for 35 to 45 minutes or till tender and no longer pink, turning once halfway through. Brush chicken with glaze frequently the last 10 minutes of grilling. Makes 4 servings.

Indirect Grilling: Preheat gas grill. Adjust the heat for indirect cooking. Place chicken, bone side down, on grill rack over medium heat. Cover and grill for 50 to 60 minutes or till no longer pink, turning once halfway through. Brush with glaze frequently the last 10 minutes of grilling.

Per serving: *323 calories, 34 g protein, 2 g carbohydrate, 20 g total fat (5 g saturated), 104 mg cholesterol, 195 mg sodium, 268 mg potassium*

Chicken with Cranberry-Orange Glaze

2 to 2½ pounds meaty chicken
    pieces (breasts, thighs,
    and drumsticks)
½ cup cranberry-orange sauce

⅓ cup orange marmalade
1 tablespoon vinegar
1 teaspoon grated gingerroot

1 Remove skin from chicken, if desired. Rinse chicken; pat dry. For glaze, in a small mixing bowl combine cranberry-orange sauce, orange marmalade, vinegar, and gingerroot. Set glaze aside.

2 Preheat gas grill. Adjust heat for direct cooking. Place chicken, bone side up, on grill rack over medium heat. Cover and grill for 35 to 45 minutes or till tender and no longer pink, turning once halfway through. Brush with glaze frequently the last 10 minutes of grilling. Makes 4 servings.

Indirect Grilling: Preheat gas grill. Adjust heat for indirect cooking. Place chicken, bone side down, on grill rack over medium heat. Cover and grill for 50 to 60 minutes or till tender and no longer pink, turning once halfway through. Brush chicken with glaze frequently the last 10 minutes of grilling.

Per serving: 350 calories, 34 g protein, 24 g carbohydrate, 13 g total fat (4 g saturated), 104 mg cholesterol, 97 mg sodium, 265 mg potassium

Tangy Chicken Breasts

**4 large boneless, skinless
  chicken breast halves
  (1 pound total)**
¼ cup orange marmalade
1 tablespoon orange juice

**¼ teaspoon finely shredded
  lime peel**
2 teaspoons lime juice
½ teaspoon grated gingerroot

*These flavorful
chicken breasts
make a super low-
fat entrée.
Complete your
healthful meal with
steamed fresh
veggies, a tossed
salad, and fresh
fruit for dessert.*

1 Rinse chicken; pat dry. For glaze, in a small mixing bowl combine orange marmalade, orange juice, lime peel, lime juice, and gingerroot.

2 Preheat gas grill. Adjust heat for direct cooking. Place chicken on grill rack over medium heat. Cover and grill for 12 to 15 minutes or till chicken is tender and no longer pink, turning once halfway through. Brush occasionally with glaze. Makes 4 servings.

Indirect Grilling: Preheat gas grill. Adjust heat for indirect cooking. Place chicken on a grill rack over medium heat. Cover and grill for 15 to 18 minutes or till tender and no longer pink, turning once halfway through. Brush occasionally with glaze.

Per serving: 147 calories, 22 g protein, 7 g carbohydrate, 3 g total fat (1 g saturated), 59 mg cholesterol, 54 mg sodium, 182 mg potassium

Microwave-to-Grill Cooking Chicken

The microwave oven and the gas grill can be teamed up to cook chicken quickly. But for safe cooking, partially cooked chicken must go directly from the microwave to the grill. So preheat your grill (and use the direct cooking method) as you precook the chicken in your microwave oven.

To microwave chicken pieces before placing them on the grill, arrange the chicken, skin side down, in a dish with the meaty portions toward the edges of the dish. Micro-cook, covered with wax paper, on 100% power (high) for 6 to 8 minutes or till no longer pink on the surface, giving the dish a half-turn after 4 minutes. Drain off the juices. Immediately place the chicken on the grill rack according to recipe directions. Cover and grill the chicken 14 to 16 minutes or till chicken is tender and no longer pink, turning once halfway through.

Chicken with Maple Glaze

A touch of bourbon adds flavor to this sweet, glistening glaze.

2 to 2½ pounds meaty chicken pieces (breasts, thighs, and drumsticks)
3 tablespoons maple syrup or maple-flavored syrup

2 tablespoons margarine or butter, melted
2 tablespoons bourbon or orange juice

1 Remove skin from chicken, if desired. Rinse chicken; pat dry. For glaze, in a small mixing bowl combine maple syrup, margarine or butter, and bourbon or orange juice.

2 Preheat gas grill. Adjust heat for direct cooking. Place chicken, bone side up, on grill rack over medium heat. Cover and grill for 35 to 45 minutes or till tender and no longer pink, turning once halfway through. Brush with glaze frequently the last 10 minutes of grilling. Makes 4 servings.

Indirect Grilling: Preheat gas grill. Adjust heat for indirect cooking. Place chicken, bone side down, on grill rack over medium heat. Cover and grill for 50 to 60 minutes or till tender and no longer pink, turning once halfway through. Brush with glaze frequently the last 10 minutes of grilling.

Per serving: 361 calories, 33 g protein, 10 g carbohydrate, 18 g total fat (5 g saturated), 104 mg cholesterol, 160 mg sodium, 277 mg potassium

Cinnamon-Peach Cornish Hens

2 1¼- to 1½-pound Cornish
  game hens, halved
  lengthwise
⅓ cup peach preserves

1 tablespoon peach nectar or
  orange juice
¼ teaspoon ground cinnamon
  Dash salt
  Dash ground ginger

If an elegant dinner for two is what you have in mind, these Cornish hens are your answer.

1 Rinse hens; pat dry. For glaze, in a small saucepan combine peach preserves, nectar or orange juice, cinnamon, salt, and ginger. Heat till the preserves melt, stirring occasionally.

2 Preheat gas grill. Adjust heat for indirect cooking. Place the hens, bone side down, on a rack in a roasting pan on the grill rack over medium heat. Cover and grill for 1 to 1¼ hours or till meat is tender and no longer pink, brushing occasionally with glaze during the last 15 minutes of grilling. Makes 2 servings.

Per serving: 723 calories, 60 g protein, 38 g carbohydrate, 38 g total fat (8 g saturated), 200 mg cholesterol, 221 mg sodium, 52 mg potassium

Orange Swordfish

Even the most devoted beefeater will go for these "meaty" (firm-textured) fish steaks.

4 6-ounce fresh or frozen
   swordfish or halibut
   steaks, cut 1 inch thick
2 tablespoons olive oil
2 tablespoons orange juice
   concentrate

1 tablespoon snipped fresh
   oregano or 1 teaspoon
   dried oregano, crushed
1 teaspoon finely shredded
   orange peel
¼ teaspoon cracked black
   pepper
   Orange slices (optional)

1 Thaw fish, if frozen. For glaze, in a small mixing bowl combine oil, orange juice concentrate, oregano, orange peel, and pepper.

2 Brush grill rack lightly with oil. Preheat gas grill. Adjust heat for direct cooking. Place swordfish on grill rack over medium heat. Cover and grill for 8 to 10 minutes or just till fish begins to flake easily, turning once halfway through and brushing occasionally with glaze. Garnish with orange slices, if desired. Makes 4 servings.

Indirect Grilling: Brush grill rack lightly with oil. Preheat gas grill. Adjust heat for indirect cooking. Place swordfish on grill rack over medium heat. Cover and grill for 8 to 12 minutes or just till fish begins to flake easily, turning once halfway through and brushing occasionally with glaze.

Per serving: 282 calories, 34 g protein, 4 g carbohydrate, 14 g total fat (3 g saturated), 67 mg cholesterol, 153 mg sodium, 556 mg potassium

Oriental Grilled Tuna

**4 6-ounce fresh or frozen tuna
  steaks, cut 1 inch thick**
**3 tablespoons olive oil or
  cooking oil**
2 tablespoons dry sherry
2 tablespoons soy sauce

1 tablespoon lemon juice
½ teaspoon toasted sesame oil
1 clove garlic, minced
**½ teaspoon grated gingerroot
  or ⅛ teaspoon ground
  ginger**
Cooking oil

*If tuna steaks
aren't available,
halibut or
marlin are good
alternatives.*

1 Thaw fish, if frozen. For glaze, in a small mixing bowl combine oil, sherry, soy sauce, lemon juice, sesame oil, garlic, and gingerroot.

2 Brush grill rack lightly with oil. Preheat gas grill. Adjust heat for direct cooking. Place tuna on grill rack over medium heat. Cover and grill for 8 to 10 minutes or just till fish begins to flake easily, turning once halfway through and brushing occasionally with glaze. Makes 4 servings.

Indirect Grilling: Brush grill rack lightly with oil. Preheat gas grill. Adjust heat for indirect cooking. Place tuna on grill rack over medium heat. Cover and grill for 8 to 12 minutes or just till fish begins to flake easily, turning once halfway through and brushing occasionally with glaze.

Per serving: 377 calories, 44 g protein, 2 g carbohydrate, 20 g total fat (4 g saturated), 71 mg cholesterol, 587 mg sodium, 497 mg potassium

Rub It with Seasoning

Rub it in, rub it in—that's just what we do in this chapter full of flavor-packed meat, poultry, and fish recipes! Combinations of seasonings and spices, rubbed directly onto the surface, add intense flavor and pleasant surprises to the main dishes in this chapter.

In This Chapter:

Roast Pork with Louisiana Rub

1 teaspoon onion powder
¼ to ½ teaspoon garlic powder
¼ to ½ teaspoon ground white
    pepper
¼ to ½ teaspoon ground red
    pepper

¼ to ½ teaspoon ground black
    pepper
¼ teaspoon salt
1 2-pound boneless pork
    top loin roast (single loin)

Down south in Cajun country, mouth-tingling rubs like this one are the favorite way to season food.

1 For rub, in a small mixing bowl combine onion powder, garlic powder, white pepper, red pepper, black pepper, and salt.

2 Trim fat from meat. Sprinkle rub mixture evenly over meat; rub in with your fingers. Insert a meat thermometer near center of roast.

3 Preheat gas grill. Adjust heat for indirect cooking. Place pork roast on a rack in a roasting pan on the grill rack over medium-low heat. Cover and grill for 1 to 1¼ hours or till meat thermometer registers 160° to 170°. Slice to serve. Makes 8 servings.

Per serving: 137 calories, 16 g protein, 0 g carbohydrate, 7 g total fat (3 g saturated), 51 mg cholesterol, 106 mg sodium, 209 mg potassium

Horseradish-Rubbed Beef Tenderloin

This sensational dish is a guaranteed crowd-pleaser.

¼ cup prepared horseradish
½ teaspoon coarsely cracked pepper
½ teaspoon finely shredded lemon peel
2 teaspoons lemon juice
3 tablespoons margarine or butter, melted

1 2½- to 3-pound beef tenderloin
⅓ cup dairy sour cream
1 tablespoon snipped fresh chives
¼ cup whipping cream, whipped

1 In a small mixing bowl combine horseradish, pepper, lemon peel, and lemon juice; reserve 2 tablespoons of the horseradish mixture. Stir melted margarine or butter into remaining horseradish mixture. Brush margarine mixture onto roast. Insert a meat thermometer into center of roast.

2 Preheat gas grill. Adjust heat for indirect cooking. Place meat on a rack in a roasting pan on the grill rack over medium-high heat. Cover and grill for 45 to 60 minutes or till meat thermometer registers 140° (rare). Let meat stand, covered, for 15 minutes. Meanwhile, for sauce, stir together reserved horseradish mixture, sour cream, and chives; fold in whipped cream.

3 Thinly slice meat across the grain. Pass sauce. Makes 10 servings.

Per serving: *226 calories, 22 g protein, 1 g carbohydrate, 14 g total fat (6 g saturated), 75 mg cholesterol, 161 mg sodium, 357 mg potassium*

Pepper-Coated Lamb Chops

8 lamb loin chops, cut 1 inch thick (about 2½ pounds total)
2 tablespoons coarse-grain brown mustard

1 tablespoon coarsely cracked black pepper
2 teaspoons soy sauce
1 clove garlic, minced

1 Trim fat from meat; set aside. In a bowl combine mustard, pepper, soy sauce, and garlic. Spread mixture evenly onto both sides of lamb chops.

2 Preheat gas grill. Adjust heat for direct cooking. Place chops on grill rack over medium heat. Cover and grill for 10 to 16 minutes or till desired doneness, turning once halfway through. Makes 4 servings.

Per serving: 624 calories, 86 g protein, 2 g carbohydrate, 28 g total fat (10 g saturated), 267 mg cholesterol, 511 mg sodium, 1,105 mg potassium

Picnics and Food Safety

To make sure the foods you tote to any summer celebrations stay safe to eat from preparation to serving, keep these hints in mind.

1. Use thermal containers and insulated coolers to keep hot foods hot (140° or more) and cold foods cold (40° or less). Always pack hot and cold foods in separate containers.

2. Pack your cooler so the foods you will eat first are on the top. This way you avoid unpacking and repacking the food.

3. Store your cooler in a shady spot. It's easy for cold foods to warm up quickly when they're sitting in the hot sunlight all day, even if they're packed in an insulated cooler.

4. Use bottled mayonnaise or salad dressing instead of homemade for sandwiches and salads. The acidity of commercial mayonnaise helps prevent food spoilage.

5. Bring only as much food as will be eaten—leftovers must be discarded.

Herb-Rubbed Rack of Lamb

If you're using dried herbs, crush them using a mortar and pestle or rub them between your fingers to release the flavor.

2 1- to 1½-pound lamb rib roasts (6 to 8 ribs each), with or without backbone
1 tablespoon olive oil or cooking oil
1 tablespoon snipped fresh mint or 1 teaspoon dried mint, crushed

1½ teaspoons snipped fresh rosemary or ½ teaspoon dried rosemary, crushed
1½ teaspoons snipped fresh oregano or ½ teaspoon dried oregano, crushed
¼ teaspoon onion salt
¼ teaspoon pepper
1 to 2 cloves garlic, minced

1 Trim fat from roasts. Brush surface of meat with oil. In a small mixing bowl combine mint, rosemary, oregano, onion salt, pepper, and garlic. Sprinkle evenly over meat; rub in with your fingers.

2 Insert a meat thermometer near center of roast, not touching bones.

3 Preheat gas grill. Adjust heat for indirect cooking. Place meat on a rack in a roasting pan on the grill rack over medium-low heat. Cover and grill to desired doneness. Allow ¾ to 1 hour for rare (140°) and 1 to 1¼ hours for medium-well (160°). Makes 4 servings.

Per serving: *277 calories, 34 g protein, 1 g carbohydrate, 14 g total fat (4 g saturated), 107 mg cholesterol, 195 mg sodium, 436 mg potassium*

Jamaican Jerk Chicken

1 2½- to 3-pound broiler-fryer chicken, cut into quarters
2 teaspoons sugar
1½ teaspoons onion powder
1½ teaspoons dried thyme, crushed
1 teaspoon ground allspice

1 teaspoon ground black pepper
½ to 1 teaspoon ground red pepper
½ teaspoon salt
¼ teaspoon ground nutmeg
⅛ teaspoon ground cloves

This rub gets its kick from ground pepper and spices.

1 Remove skin from chicken, if desired. Rinse chicken; pat dry. For rub, in a small mixing bowl combine sugar, onion powder, thyme, allspice, black pepper, red pepper, salt, nutmeg, and cloves. Sprinkle evenly over chicken; rub in with your fingers.

2 Preheat gas grill. Adjust heat for direct cooking. Place chicken, bone side up, on grill rack over medium heat. Cover and grill for 40 to 50 minutes or till chicken is tender and no longer pink, turning once halfway through. Makes 4 servings.

Indirect Grilling: Preheat gas grill. Adjust heat for indirect cooking. Place chicken, bone side down, on grill rack over medium heat. Cover and grill for 50 to 60 minutes or till chicken is tender and no longer pink, turning once halfway through.

Per serving: 284 calories, 31 g protein, 4 g carbohydrate, 15 g total fat (4 g saturated), 99 mg cholesterol, 360 mg sodium, 278 mg potassium

Turkey Drumsticks with Sesame Rub

Slice the meat off the turkey drumsticks before serving.

**2 turkey drumsticks
(1 to 1½ pounds total) or
8 chicken drumsticks
(about 1½ pounds total)**
**3 tablespoons very thinly sliced
green onion**
1 tablespoon sesame seed

**1½ teaspoons toasted sesame
oil**
1 teaspoon grated gingerroot
¼ teaspoon salt
Dash ground red pepper
1 clove garlic, minced

1 Remove skin from turkey or chicken drumsticks. Rinse turkey or chicken; pat dry.

2 For rub, in a small mixing bowl combine green onion, sesame seed, sesame oil, gingerroot, salt, pepper, and garlic. Spread rub mixture evenly over turkey or chicken.

3 Preheat gas grill. Adjust heat for indirect cooking. Place turkey on a rack in a pan. Place the pan on the grill rack over medium heat. (Place chicken directly on the grill rack.) Cover and grill for 45 minutes to 1¼ hours for turkey or 35 to 40 minutes for chicken or till poultry is tender and no longer pink. Makes 4 servings.

Per serving: *130 calories, 18 g protein, 1 g carbohydrate, 6 g total fat
(1 g saturated), 42 mg cholesterol, 182 mg sodium, 169 mg potassium*

Chili-Rubbed Chicken

2 to 2½ pounds meaty chicken
   pieces (breasts, thighs,
   and drumsticks)
1½ teaspoons paprika
½ teaspoon ground cumin
½ teaspoon chili powder

¼ to ½ teaspoon ground black
   pepper
¼ to ½ teaspoon ground red
   pepper
¼ teaspoon ground coriander
¼ teaspoon salt

1 Remove skin from chicken, if desired. Rinse chicken; pat dry. For rub, in a small mixing bowl combine paprika, cumin, chili powder, black pepper, red pepper, coriander, and salt. Sprinkle evenly over chicken; rub in with your fingers.

2 Preheat gas grill. Adjust heat for direct cooking. Place chicken, bone side up, on grill rack over medium heat. Cover and grill for 35 to 45 minutes or till chicken is tender and no longer pink, turning once halfway through. Makes 4 servings.

Indirect Grilling: Preheat gas grill. Adjust heat for indirect cooking. Place chicken, bone side down, on grill rack over medium heat. Cover and grill for 50 to 60 minutes or till chicken is tender and no longer pink, turning once halfway through.

Per serving: 262 calories, 34 g protein, 1 g carbohydrate, 13 g total fat (4 g saturated), 104 mg cholesterol, 229 mg sodium, 283 mg potassium

Seasoned Fish Steaks

4 6-ounce fresh or frozen
   salmon or halibut steaks,
   cut 1 inch thick
2 tablespoons margarine or
   butter, softened
3 tablespoons horseradish
   mustard or Dijon-style
   mustard

1 tablespoon snipped fresh dill
   or 1 teaspoon dried
   dillweed
¼ teaspoon coarsely cracked
   black pepper

1 Thaw fish, if frozen. In a small mixing bowl combine softened margarine or butter, mustard, dill, and pepper. Spread mixture evenly over both sides of fish steaks.

2 Brush grill rack lightly with oil. Preheat gas grill. Adjust heat for direct cooking. Place fish steaks on grill rack over medium heat. Cover and grill 8 to 10 minutes or just till fish begins to flake easily, turning once halfway through. Makes 4 servings.

Indirect Grilling: Brush grill rack lightly with oil. Preheat gas grill. Adjust heat for indirect cooking. Place fish steaks on grill rack over medium heat. Cover and grill 8 to 12 minutes or just till fish begins to flake easily, turning once halfway through.

Per serving: 217 calories, 25 g protein, 1 g carbohydrate, 12 g total fat (2 g saturated), 31 mg cholesterol, 272 mg sodium, 249 mg potassium

Cajun-Coated Fish

4 fresh or frozen catfish, red
    snapper, or haddock fillets,
    ½ to ¾ inch thick
    (1 to 1¼ pounds)
¼ cup all-purpose flour
¼ cup yellow cornmeal
1 teaspoon dried basil,
    crushed
1 teaspoon onion powder
½ to 1 teaspoon ground red
    pepper

½ teaspoon garlic salt
½ teaspoon ground white
    pepper
½ teaspoon dried thyme,
    crushed
¼ to ½ teaspoon ground black
    pepper
¼ teaspoon ground sage
¼ cup margarine or butter

Mix a pitcher of margaritas to cool the heat from these highly seasoned fish fillets.

1 Thaw fish, if frozen. In a shallow mixing bowl combine flour, cornmeal, basil, onion powder, red pepper, garlic salt, white pepper, thyme, black pepper, and sage. Coat both sides of the fish with the flour mixture.

2 Turn gas grill to high heat. Place a 12-inch cast-iron or oven-going skillet on the grill rack; add margarine. Cover and heat for 1 to 2 minutes or till margarine is bubbly.

3 Add fish to skillet. Cover and grill for 6 to 8 minutes or till golden. Turn the fish. Cover and grill for 6 to 8 minutes more or just till fish begins to flake easily and coating is crispy. Makes 4 servings.

Per serving: 278 calories, 25 g protein, 13 g carbohydrate, 13 g total fat (3 g saturated), 42 mg cholesterol, 441 mg sodium, 508 mg potassium

Make It with Marinade

Grill favorites take on new life with the savory marinades in this chapter. From apple to beer to dill, these taste-tempting marinades are an easy way to tenderize and add outstanding flavor to your main course.

In This Chapter:

Marinated Steak

1 1½-pound beef top round
   steak, cut 1 inch thick
1 teaspoon finely shredded
   lemon peel
⅓ cup lemon juice
¼ cup cooking oil
4 teaspoons Worcestershire
   sauce
1 tablespoon snipped fresh basil
   or 1 teaspoon dried basil,
   crushed

1 tablespoon snipped fresh
   thyme or 1 teaspoon
   dried thyme, crushed
1 tablespoon honey
½ teaspoon coarsely ground
   black pepper
¼ teaspoon salt
2 cloves garlic, minced

Why do we recommend marinating foods in a plastic bag placed in a bowl? Because it's less messy and much easier to keep the food covered with the marinade!

1 Slash fat edges of steak at 1 inch intervals. Place meat in a plastic bag set in a shallow dish. For marinade, combine lemon peel, lemon juice, oil, Worcestershire sauce, basil, thyme, honey, pepper, salt, and garlic. Pour over steak. Close bag. Marinate in refrigerator for 6 to 24 hours, turning occasionally.

2 Drain steak, reserving marinade. Preheat gas grill. Adjust heat for direct cooking. Place steak on grill rack over medium heat. Cover and grill to desired doneness, turning once halfway through and brushing occasionally with reserved marinade. (Allow 14 to 16 minutes for rare and 18 to 20 minutes for medium.)

3 To serve, thinly slice meat across the grain. Makes 6 servings.

Indirect Grilling: Preheat gas grill. Adjust heat for indirect cooking. Place steak on grill rack over medium heat. Cover and grill to desired doneness, turning once halfway through and brushing occasionally with reserved marinade. (Allow 24 to 26 minutes for rare and 28 to 30 minutes for medium.)

Per serving: 213 calories, 27 g protein, 2 g carbohydrate, 10 g total fat (3 g saturated), 72 mg cholesterol, 117 mg sodium, 399 mg potassium

Grilled London Broil

1 1- to 1½-pound beef flank
   steak or top round steak
3 tablespoons red wine vinegar
3 tablespoons cooking oil

3 cloves garlic, minced
1 teaspoon coarsely ground
   pepper
¼ teaspoon salt

1 Score meat by making shallow cuts at 1-inch intervals diagonally across steak in a diamond pattern. Repeat scoring on second side. Place meat in a plastic bag set in a shallow dish.

2 For marinade, combine vinegar, oil, garlic, pepper, and salt. Pour marinade over steak. Close bag. Marinate in refrigerator for 6 to 24 hours, turning occasionally.

3 Drain steak, reserving marinade. Preheat gas grill. Adjust heat for direct cooking. Place meat on grill rack over medium heat. Cover and grill 12 to 14 minutes or till desired doneness, turning once halfway through and brushing occasionally with reserved marinade.

4 To serve, thinly slice steak diagonally across the grain. Makes 4 to 6 servings.

Indirect Grilling: Preheat gas grill. Adjust heat for indirect grilling. Place meat on grill rack over medium heat. Cover and grill for 18 to 22 minutes or till desired doneness, turning once halfway through and brushing occasionally with reserved marinade. Continue as directed above.

Per serving: 214 calories, 22 g protein, 1 g carbohydrate, 13 g total fat (4 g saturated), 53 mg cholesterol, 133 mg sodium, 344 mg potassium

Beer-Marinated Beef

1 3- to 4-pound boneless sirloin
   roast
1 cup beer
1 tablespoon brown sugar
2 teaspoons Worcestershire
   sauce

1 teaspoon onion salt
½ teaspoon dry mustard
1 teaspoon seasoned salt
½ teaspoon paprika
½ teaspoon pepper

1 Trim fat from meat. Place roast in a plastic bag set in a shallow dish. For marinade, combine beer, brown sugar, Worcestershire sauce, onion salt, and dry mustard; pour over roast. Close bag. Marinate in refrigerator for 12 to 24 hours, turning occasionally. Drain meat, reserving marinade.

2 In a custard cup combine seasoned salt, paprika, and pepper; sprinkle over both sides of roast.

3 Preheat gas grill. Adjust heat for indirect cooking. Place roast on a rack in a pan on grill rack over slow heat. Cover and grill to desired doneness, brushing with reserved marinade every 30 minutes. Allow 1 to 2 hours for rare and 2 to 2½ hours for medium.

4 To serve, thinly slice roast diagonally across the grain. Makes 10 servings.

Per serving: *250 calories, 31 g protein, 1 g carbohydrate, 12 g total fat (5 g saturated), 91 mg cholesterol, 154 mg sodium, 419 mg potassium*

Brushing with Marinades

When brushing with a reserved marinade used for meat, poultry, or fish, do not brush it on during the last 5 minutes of grilling. The marinade has raw meat juices in it that need to be thoroughly cooked.

Apple-Thyme Marinated Chops

In your supermarket, these thick pork chops are often labeled "Iowa Chops."

4 **pork loin or rib chops, cut 1¼ inches thick (about 2¼ pounds total)**
1 **6-ounce can frozen apple juice concentrate, thawed**
2 **tablespoons cooking oil**

1 **tablespoon snipped fresh thyme or 1 teaspoon dried thyme, crushed**
1 **tablespoon honey**
1 **tablespoon soy sauce**

1 Trim fat from meat. Place chops in a plastic bag set in a deep bowl. For marinade, combine apple juice concentrate, oil, thyme, honey, and soy sauce. Pour marinade over chops. Close bag. Marinate in refrigerator for 6 to 24 hours, turning occasionally. Drain chops, reserving marinade.

2 Preheat gas grill. Adjust heat for indirect cooking. Place chops on grill rack over medium heat. Cover and grill for 35 to 40 minutes or till juices run clear, turning once halfway through and brushing occasionally with reserved marinade. Makes 4 servings.

Per serving: *281 calories, 22 g protein, 15 g carbohydrate, 15 g total fat (4 g saturated), 68 mg cholesterol, 232 mg sodium, 409 mg potassium*

Mediterranean Marinated Lamb

1 3½- to 4-pound boneless leg
   of lamb, rolled and tied
⅓ cup olive oil or cooking oil
3 tablespoons wine vinegar
3 tablespoons tarragon vinegar
¼ cup finely chopped onion
2 cloves garlic, minced

1 tablespoon snipped fresh
   oregano or 1 teaspoon
   dried oregano, crushed
1 tablespoon snipped fresh
   rosemary or 1 teaspoon
   dried rosemary, crushed
½ teaspoon salt

The garlic, olive oil, and combination of fresh herbs give this leg of lamb a real Mediterranean flavor.

1 Untie meat; trim fat. Place lamb in a plastic bag set in a shallow dish. For marinade, combine oil, wine vinegar, tarragon vinegar, onion, garlic, oregano, rosemary, and salt; pour marinade over lamb. Close bag. Marinate in refrigerator for 6 to 24 hours, turning occasionally.

2 Drain lamb, reserving marinade. Reroll and tie lamb. Insert a meat thermometer near center of roast.

3 Preheat gas grill. Adjust heat for indirect cooking. Place lamb on a rack in a roasting pan on the grill rack over medium heat. Cover and grill for 2¼ to 3 hours or till meat thermometer registers 140° (rare) to 160° (medium-well), brushing occasionally with reserved marinade during the first 2 hours.

4 To serve, remove strings and slice. Makes 14 to 16 servings.

Per serving: 191 calories, 17 g protein, 1 g carbohydrate, 13 g total fat (5 g saturated), 60 mg cholesterol, 119 mg sodium, 212 mg potassium

Wine-Marinated Lamb Chops

8 lamb loin chops, cut 1 inch thick (about 2½ pounds total)

⅓ cup dry red wine

¼ cup chopped onion

2 tablespoons olive oil

1 tablespoon snipped fresh rosemary or ½ teaspoon dried rosemary, crushed

1 tablespoon snipped fresh basil or ½ teaspoon dried basil, crushed

1½ teaspoons snipped fresh oregano or ¼ teaspoon dried oregano, crushed

1½ teaspoons snipped fresh thyme or ¼ teaspoon dried thyme, crushed

1 teaspoon Dijon-style mustard

¼ teaspoon pepper

1 Trim fat from meat. Place chops in a plastic bag set in a deep bowl. For marinade, in a small mixing bowl combine wine, onion, oil, rosemary, basil, oregano, thyme, mustard, and pepper. Pour marinade over chops. Close bag. Marinate in refrigerator for 6 to 24 hours, turning occasionally.

2 Drain chops, discarding marinade. Preheat gas grill. Adjust heat for direct cooking. Place lamb chops on grill rack over medium heat. Cover and grill for 10 to 16 minutes or till desired doneness, turning once. Makes 4 servings.

Indirect Grilling: Preheat gas grill. Adjust heat for indirect cooking. Place chops on grill rack over medium heat. Cover and grill for 16 to 20 minutes or till desired doneness, turning once.

Per serving: 262 calories, 32 g protein, 0 g carbohydrate, 13 g total fat (5 g saturated), 104 mg cholesterol, 91 mg sodium, 334 mg potassium

Salmon with Citrus Marinade

4 6-ounce fresh or frozen
salmon or halibut steaks,
cut 1 inch thick
¼ cup frozen orange juice
concentrate, thawed

2 tablespoons cooking oil
2 teaspoons finely shredded
lemon peel
2 tablespoons lemon juice
2 cloves garlic, minced

A delightful orange and lemon combination flavors these fish steaks.

1 Thaw fish, if frozen. Place fish in a plastic bag set in a deep bowl. For marinade, mix orange juice concentrate, oil, lemon peel, lemon juice, and garlic. Pour marinade over salmon. Close bag. Marinate in refrigerator for 2 hours, turning occasionally. Drain salmon, reserving marinade.

2 Brush grill rack lightly with oil. Preheat gas grill. Adjust heat for indirect cooking. Place salmon on grill rack over medium heat. Cover and grill for 8 to 12 minutes or just till fish begins to flake easily, brushing with reserved marinade and turning once halfway through. Makes 4 servings.

Per serving: 201 calories, 25 g protein, 4 g carbohydrate, 9 g total fat (2 g saturated), 31 mg cholesterol, 105 mg sodium, 301 mg potassium

Tex-Mex Marinated Chicken

Hosting a Mexican-inspired barbecue? Use a cactus for your center-piece and add colorful placemats and napkins.

2 to 2½ pounds meaty chicken pieces (breasts, thighs, and drumsticks)
¼ cup lime juice
¼ cup orange juice
3 tablespoons snipped fresh cilantro

3 tablespoons olive oil or cooking oil
1 tablespoon chili powder
1½ teaspoons ground cumin
½ teaspoon salt
½ teaspoon bottled hot pepper sauce
2 cloves garlic, minced

1 Remove skin from chicken, if desired. Rinse chicken; pat dry. Place the chicken in a plastic bag set in a deep bowl. For marinade, combine lime juice, orange juice, cilantro, oil, chili powder, cumin, salt, hot pepper sauce, and garlic; pour over chicken. Close bag. Marinate in refrigerator for 6 to 24 hours, turning occasionally.

2 Drain chicken, reserving marinade.

3 Preheat gas grill. Adjust heat for indirect cooking. Place chicken, bone side down, on a grill rack over medium heat. Cover and grill for 50 to 60 minutes or till chicken is tender and no longer pink, turning once halfway through and brushing occasionally with reserved marinade before turning. Makes 4 servings.

Per serving: 322 calories, 33 g protein, 5 g carbohydrate, 18 g total fat (4 g saturated), 100 mg cholesterol, 385 mg sodium, 393 mg potassium

Tandoori Chicken

2 to 2½ pounds meaty chicken pieces (breasts, thighs, and drumsticks)
2 8-ounce cartons plain yogurt
3 tablespoons lemon juice
1 tablespoon grated gingerroot
2 teaspoons paprika

1 teaspoon ground cumin
1 teaspoon ground coriander
½ teaspoon salt
½ teaspoon ground turmeric
¼ teaspoon ground red pepper
2 cloves garlic, minced
Chutney (optional)

1 Remove skin from chicken, if desired. Rinse chicken; pat dry. Place chicken in a plastic bag set in a deep bowl. For marinade, combine yogurt, lemon juice, gingerroot, paprika, cumin, coriander, salt, turmeric, red pepper, and garlic; pour over chicken. Close bag. Marinate in refrigerator for 6 to 24 hours, turning occasionally.

2 Drain chicken, reserving marinade. (Chill reserved marinade while grilling chicken.)

3 Preheat gas grill. Adjust heat for indirect cooking. Place chicken, bone side down, on grill rack over medium heat. Cover and grill for 50 to 60 minutes or till chicken is tender and no longer pink, turning once halfway through and brushing with marinade the last half of grilling. Serve with chutney, if desired. Makes 4 servings.

Per serving: 292 calories, 37 g protein, 6 g carbohydrate, 13 g total fat (4 g saturated), 105 mg cholesterol, 266 mg sodium, 420 mg potassium

In India, a "tandoor" is a large clay oven which quickly roasts meats with intense heat. The combination of the traditional spicy yogurt marinade and the tandoor method of cooking produces foods with a characteristic bright reddish-orange color.

Chicken Salad with Apples and Nuts

Is washing lettuce a dreaded chore at your house? Look for bags of prewashed mixed greens in the produce section of your supermarket.

4 large boneless, skinless chicken breast halves (1 pound total)
¼ cup apple juice concentrate, thawed
2 tablespoons cooking oil
2 tablespoons soy sauce
1 tablespoon white wine vinegar
1 tablespoon snipped fresh summer savory or 1 teaspoon dried savory, crushed

½ cup mayonnaise or salad dressing
3 tablespoons apple juice concentrate, thawed
1 tablespoon coarse-grain brown mustard
¼ teaspoon salt
¼ teaspoon pepper
6 cups torn mixed greens
2 medium apples, cored and sliced
Spiced Nuts

1 Rinse chicken; pat dry. Place in a plastic bag set in a shallow dish. For marinade, combine the ¼ cup thawed apple juice concentrate, oil, soy sauce, vinegar, and savory. Pour over chicken. Close bag. Marinate in refrigerator for 6 to 24 hours, turning occasionally.

2 Meanwhile, for dressing, in a mixing bowl combine mayonnaise, the 3 tablespoons juice concentrate, mustard, salt, and pepper. Cover and chill.

3 Drain chicken, reserving marinade. Preheat gas grill. Adjust heat for direct cooking. Place chicken on grill rack over medium heat. Cover and grill for 12 to 15 minutes or till chicken is tender and no longer pink, turning once halfway through; brush occasionally with reserved marinade. Discard any remaining marinade. Cut chicken diagonally into ½-inch-wide strips.

4 Divide mixed greens among 4 plates. Reassemble breast halves atop greens. Fan apple slices around chicken breasts. Spoon dressing over salads. Sprinkle with Spiced Nuts. Makes 4 servings.

Spiced Nuts: Combine ¾ cup broken *pecans or walnuts;* 1 tablespoon *margarine or butter,* melted; ¼ teaspoon *ground cumin;* ⅛ teaspoon *ground red pepper;* and dash *salt.* Bake in a 350° oven about 10 minutes or till light brown, stirring once or twice. Cool.

Per serving: 590 calories, 25 g protein, 23 g carbohydrate, 46 g total fat (6 g saturated), 75 mg cholesterol, 702 mg sodium, 633 mg potassium

Spicy Mini-Drumstick Appetizers

24 chicken wings	**1 tablespoon honey**
¼ cup soy sauce	**½ teaspoon onion powder**
¼ cup dry sherry	**½ teaspoon five-spice powder**
2 tablespoons cooking oil	**1 cup sweet-and-sour sauce**

1 For mini drumsticks, bend the 2 larger sections of each chicken wing back and forth, breaking the cartilage that connects the larger wing portion (the mini drumstick) with the 2-part wing-tip section. Use a knife or cleaver to cut through the skin and cartilage that connects the 2 larger sections of each wing. (Reserve 2-part wing-tip section to make stock or soup.) Use the tip of a small knife to cut cartilage loose from the cut end of each mini drumstick. Push meat and skin to top of bone, shaping it into a compact ball. Place mini drumsticks in a plastic bag set in a deep bowl.

2 For marinade, combine soy sauce, sherry, oil, honey, onion powder, and five-spice powder. Pour marinade over chicken. Close bag. Marinate in refrigerator for 6 to 24 hours, turning occasionally.

3 Drain mini drumsticks, reserving marinade. Preheat gas grill. Adjust heat for direct cooking. Place mini drumsticks on grill rack over medium-low heat. Cover and grill for 15 to 20 minutes or till tender and no longer pink, turning once halfway through and brushing frequently with reserved marinade. Serve with sweet-and-sour sauce. Makes 24.

Per drumstick: *132 calories, 9 g protein, 5 g carbohydrate, 8 g total fat (2 g saturated), 29 mg cholesterol, 233 mg sodium, 74 mg potassium*

These miniature drumsticks, made from the thickest section of a chicken wing, make a super summertime hors d'oeuvre at your next grill-out.

Chicken with Hoisin Marinade

Hoisin sauce, with it's sweet and piquant flavor, is a staple in Oriental cooking. It's a thick, reddish brown sauce made from soybeans, salt, sugar, garlic, flour, vinegar, and spices.

1 1½- to 3-pound broiler-fryer chicken, cut into quarters
⅓ cup hoisin sauce
⅓ cup orange juice
2 tablespoons thinly sliced green onion
1 tablespoon white vinegar
1 tablespoon honey
1 teaspoon toasted sesame oil
2 cloves garlic, minced

1 Remove skin from chicken, if desired. Rinse chicken; pat dry. Place in a plastic bag set in a deep bowl. For marinade, combine hoisin sauce, orange juice, green onion, vinegar, honey, sesame oil, and garlic; pour over chicken. Close bag. Marinate in refrigerator for 6 to 24 hours, turning occasionally.

2 Drain chicken, reserving marinade. Preheat gas grill. Adjust heat for indirect cooking. Place chicken, bone side down, on grill rack over medium heat. Cover and grill for 50 to 60 minutes or till chicken is tender and no longer pink, brushing with reserved marinade and turning once halfway through. Makes 4 servings.

Per serving: 281 calories, 31 g protein, 2 g carbohydrate, 16 g total fat (4 g saturated), 99 mg cholesterol, 395 mg sodium, 273 mg potassium

Marinating Pointers

All the recipes in this chapter call for marinating foods in a plastic bag. Why? Because it usually takes less marinade and the bag makes it easy to distribute the marinade over the food. Here are other pointers to keep in mind.

● Use a heavy-duty plastic bag. Set it in a bowl in case the bag should leak.
● Marinate foods in the refrigerator—never let them stand at room temperature.
● If you have enough marinade, you can marinate foods in a glass or plastic bowl instead of a bag. But don't use a metal bowl because any acid in the marinade can pit the bowl and add an off-flavor to the marinade.
● Any leftover marinade that is to be served with your food must be heated to boiling before serving because of the raw meat juices in it.

Easy Marinated Turkey Steaks

4 turkey breast tenderloin
  steaks (about 1 pound
  total)
½ cup creamy French salad
  dressing

2 teaspoons Worcestershire
  sauce
1 teaspoon lemon juice

A tangy marinade based on bottled salad dressing keeps these turkey cuts very moist and tender.

1 Rinse turkey; pat dry. Place turkey in a plastic bag set in a shallow bowl. For marinade, stir together French salad dressing, Worcestershire sauce, and lemon juice; pour over turkey steaks. Close bag. Marinate in refrigerator for 6 to 24 hours, turning occasionally.

2 Drain turkey, reserving marinade. Preheat gas grill. Adjust heat for direct cooking. Place turkey on grill rack over medium heat. Cover and grill for 12 to 15 minutes or till turkey is tender and no longer pink, brushing with reserved marinade and turning once halfway through. Makes 4 servings.

Indirect Grilling: Preheat gas grill. Adjust heat for indirect cooking. Place turkey on grill rack over medium heat. Cover and grill for 15 to 18 minutes or till tender and no longer pink, brushing with reserved marinade and turning once halfway through.

Per serving: 248 calories, 22 g protein, 6 g carbohydrate, 15 g total fat (4 g saturated), 53 mg cholesterol, 504 mg sodium, 253 mg potassium

Stick It on a Skewer

If you can poke it or thread it, then you can grill it "enbrochette". This sizzling assortment of kabobs mixes meats, poultry, and fish and seafood with chunks of fresh fruits and vegetables for creative combinations with pizazz.

In This Chapter:

Teriyaki Beef Kabobs

1 **pound boneless beef sirloin steak, cut 1 inch thick**
1 **8¼-ounce can pineapple chunks**
3 **tablespoons soy sauce**
1 **tablespoon brown sugar**
1 **tablespoon cooking oil**

1 **clove garlic, minced**
1 **teaspoon grated gingerroot**
¼ **teaspoon pepper**
1 **medium sweet red and/or green pepper, cut into 1-inch pieces**
½ **teaspoon sesame seed**

Teriyaki refers to a Japanese dish of beef or chicken that's been marinated in a mixture of soy sauce, sugar, and ginger. The sugar in the marinade gives these kabobs a shiny glaze.

1 Trim fat from meat. Cut meat into 1-inch pieces. Place meat in a plastic bag set in a deep bowl. For marinade, drain pineapple chunks, reserving juices. Combine reserved pineapple juice, soy sauce, brown sugar, oil, garlic, gingerroot, and pepper; stir till sugar dissolves. Pour marinade over meat. Close bag. Marinate in refrigerator for 2 to 8 hours, turning occasionally.

2 Drain beef, reserving marinade. On 4 long metal skewers, alternately thread beef, sweet pepper, and pineapple chunks, leaving about ¼ inch between pieces.

3 Preheat gas grill. Adjust heat for direct cooking. Place kabobs on grill rack over medium heat. Cover and grill for 12 to 14 minutes or till beef is desired doneness, brushing with reserved marinade and turning once halfway through. Sprinkle with sesame seed the last 5 minutes of grilling. Makes 4 servings.

Indirect Grilling: Preheat gas grill. Adjust heat for indirect cooking. Place kabobs on grill rack over medium heat. Cover and grill for 16 to 18 minutes or till beef is desired doneness, brushing with reserved marinade and turning once halfway through. Sprinkle with sesame seed the last 5 minutes of grilling.

Per serving: 253 calories, 27 g protein, 8 g carbohydrate, 12 g total fat (4 g saturated), 76 mg cholesterol, 402 mg sodium, 433 mg potassium

Lamb Shish Kabobs

Choose a portion of a leg of lamb or a lamb leg sirloin chop to cut into pieces for these marinated kabobs.

1 **pound lean boneless lamb or beef sirloin**
½ **cup chopped onion**
¼ **cup lemon juice**
2 **tablespoons olive oil or cooking oil**
2 **tablespoons water**
1 **tablespoon snipped fresh oregano or 1 teaspoon dried oregano, crushed**
1 **teaspoon snipped fresh thyme or ¼ teaspoon dried thyme, crushed**

½ **teaspoon salt**
¼ **teaspoon pepper**
1 **clove garlic, minced**
2 **small red onions, cut into wedges**
1 **medium sweet red and/or green pepper, cut into 1-inch pieces**
16 **whole fresh mushrooms**
8 **cherry tomatoes (optional)**

1 Trim fat from meat. Cut lamb or beef into 1-inch pieces. Place meat in a plastic bag set in a deep bowl. For marinade, combine the chopped onion, lemon juice, oil, water, oregano, thyme, salt, pepper, and garlic. Pour marinade over lamb or beef. Close bag. Marinate in refrigerator for 2 to 8 hours, turning occasionally.

2 Meanwhile, cook red onion wedges, covered, in a small amount of boiling water for 5 minutes; drain. Drain lamb, reserving marinade. On 8 long metal skewers, alternately thread lamb, red onion wedges, pepper pieces, and mushrooms, leaving about ¼ inch between pieces.

3 Preheat gas grill. Adjust heat for direct cooking. Place kabobs on grill rack over medium heat. Cover and grill for 12 to 14 minutes or till meat is desired doneness, brushing with reserved marinade and turning kabobs once halfway through. Add a cherry tomato to each skewer the last 1 to 2 minutes of grilling, if desired. Makes 4 servings.

Indirect Grilling: Preheat gas grill. Adjust heat for indirect cooking. Place kabobs on a grill rack over medium heat. Cover and grill for 16 to 18 minutes or till meat is desired doneness, brushing with reserved marinade and turning kabobs once halfway through. Add a cherry tomato to each skewer the last 1 to 2 minutes of grilling, if desired.

Per serving: 203 calories, 20 g protein, 11 g carbohydrate, 9 g total fat (2 g saturated), 57 mg cholesterol, 182 mg sodium, 523 mg potassium

Surf 'N' Turf Kabobs

8 ounces boneless beef sirloin steak, cut 1 inch thick
⅓ cup lemon juice
¼ cup cooking oil
¼ cup white wine Worcestershire sauce
1 tablespoon honey
1½ teaspoons snipped fresh basil or ½ teaspoon dried basil, crushed
1½ teaspoons snipped fresh thyme or ½ teaspoon dried thyme, crushed

¼ teaspoon coarsely cracked black pepper
⅛ teaspoon garlic salt
8 ounces fresh or frozen large shrimp in shells (10 to 16)
1 medium onion, cut into 8 wedges
1 small zucchini, cut into ½-inch-thick slices
1 medium sweet red or orange pepper, cut into 1-inch pieces

The best of both worlds—shrimp and beef strips cooked together on the same skewer.

1 Partially freeze beef. Thinly slice across the grain into ¼-inch-thick strips. Place strips in a plastic bag set in a shallow dish. For marinade, combine lemon juice, oil, Worcestershire sauce, honey, basil, thyme, pepper, and garlic salt. Pour half of the marinade over beef strips. Close bag. Marinate in refrigerator for 3 to 4 hours, turning occasionally. Refrigerate remaining marinade.

2 Thaw shrimp, if frozen. Peel and devein shrimp, keeping tails intact.

3 Meanwhile, cook onion, covered, in a small amount of boiling water for 3 minutes. Add zucchini and cook 2 minutes more. Drain.

4 Drain beef, discarding marinade. On 8 long metal skewers, alternately thread beef, shrimp, and vegetables, leaving about ¼ inch between the pieces.

5 Preheat gas grill. Adjust heat for direct cooking. Place kabobs on grill rack over medium heat. Cover and grill for 10 to 12 minutes or till shrimp turn opaque and meat is desired doneness, turning once and brushing with chilled marinade often. Makes 4 servings.

Per serving: 231 calories, 21 g protein, 10 g carbohydrate, 12 g total fat (3 g saturated), 103 g cholesterol, 234 mg sodium, 413 mg potassium

Dill Sauced Salmon-Scallop Kabobs

¾ **pound boneless, skinless fresh or frozen salmon fillet**
8 **ounces fresh or frozen sea scallops**
½ **cup dry white wine**
¼ **cup olive oil or cooking oil**
¼ **cup lime juice**
1 **tablespoon Dijon-style mustard**

1 **teaspoon snipped fresh dill or ¼ teaspoon dried dillweed**
2 **medium carrots, cut into 1-inch chunks**
2 **small zucchini, cut into 1-inch-thick slices**
Dill Sauce

1 Thaw salmon and scallops, if frozen. Cut salmon fillet into 5 x 1½-inch strips. Set salmon strips and sea scallops in a plastic bag set in a deep bowl. For marinade, combine wine, oil, lime juice, mustard, and dill; pour over salmon and scallops. Close bag. Marinate in refrigerator for 1 to 2 hours, turning occasionally.

2 Meanwhile, in a medium saucepan cook carrots, covered, in a small amount of boiling water for 4 minutes. Add zucchini and cook 2 minutes more or till vegetables are crisp-tender. Drain.

3 Drain salmon and scallops, reserving marinade. On 4 long metal skewers, alternately thread salmon strips, zucchini, scallops, and carrots, leaving about ¼ inch between pieces.

4 Brush grill rack lightly with oil. Preheat gas grill. Adjust heat for indirect cooking. Place kabobs on grill rack over medium heat. Cover and grill for 8 to 10 minutes or till salmon just flakes with a fork and scallops turn opaque, turning kabobs once and brushing with reserved marinade halfway through.

5 Serve kabobs with Dill Sauce. Makes 4 servings.

Dill Sauce: In a small bowl combine one 8-ounce carton dairy *sour cream*, 2 tablespoons snipped fresh *dill* or 2 teaspoons *dried dillweed*, 1 tablespoon snipped fresh *chives*, 1 tablespoon *white wine vinegar*, ⅛ teaspoon *salt*, and ⅛ teaspoon *pepper*.

Per serving: 332 calories, 22 g protein, 10 g carbohydrate, 22 g total fat (9 g saturated), 57 mg cholesterol, 306 mg sodium, 571 mg potassium

Swordfish Kabobs with Fruit

1 **pound fresh or frozen swordfish, tuna, or shark steaks, cut 1 inch thick**
½ **teaspoon finely shredded orange peel**
¼ **cup orange juice**
2 **tablespoons dry sherry**
2 **tablespoons cooking oil**
1 **clove garlic, minced**

¼ **teaspoon salt**
¼ **teaspoon coarsely cracked pepper**
8 **green onions, cut into 2-inch pieces**
4 **small fresh plums, pitted and cut into quarters**
1 **medium orange, cut into chunks**

Swordfish, tuna, and shark make great kabobs because of their firm flesh.

1 Thaw fish, if frozen; cut into 1-inch cubes. Place fish in a plastic bag set in a shallow dish. For marinade, combine orange peel, orange juice, sherry, oil, garlic, salt, and pepper; pour over fish. Close bag. Marinate in refrigerator for 4 to 6 hours, turning occasionally.

2 Drain fish, reserving marinade. On 8 long metal skewers, alternately thread fish cubes, green onions, plums, and orange chunks, leaving about ¼ inch between pieces.

3 Brush grill rack lightly with oil. Preheat gas grill. Adjust heat for direct cooking. Place kabobs on grill rack over medium-hot heat. Brush kabobs with reserved marinade. Cover and grill for 8 to 12 minutes or till fish just flakes with a fork, turning once halfway through. Makes 4 servings.

Per serving: *253 calories, 23 g protein, 11 g carbohydrate, 12 g total fat (2 g saturated), 45 mg cholesterol, 236 mg sodium, 497 mg potassium*

Cajun Seafood Kabobs

12 ounces fresh or frozen large shrimp in shells (about 16)
8 ounces fresh or frozen sea scallops (about 12)
¼ cup margarine or butter
¼ teaspoon dried oregano, crushed
½ teaspoon chili powder
¼ teaspoon ground cumin
⅛ teaspoon dried thyme, crushed
⅛ teaspoon ground white pepper
⅛ teaspoon ground black pepper
Dash ground red pepper

1 Thaw shrimp and scallops, if frozen. Peel and devein shrimp, keeping tails intact. For sauce, in a small saucepan melt margarine or butter. Stir in oregano, chili powder, cumin, thyme, white pepper, black pepper, and ground red pepper. Cook for 1 minute. Set sauce aside.

2 On 8 long metal skewers, alternately thread shrimp and scallops, leaving about ¼ inch between each. Brush kabobs with sauce.

3 Preheat gas grill. Adjust heat for indirect cooking. Place kabobs on grill rack over medium heat. Cover and grill for 6 to 8 minutes or till shrimp and scallops turn opaque, brushing with sauce and turning once halfway through. Makes 4 servings.

Per serving: 223 calories, 25 g protein, 2 g carbohydrate, 13 g total fat (2 g saturated), 139 mg cholesterol, 412 mg sodium, 390 mg potassium

Preventing Flare-Ups On Your Gas Grill

It's a good idea after every use to turn your gas grill on HIGH and let it run for 10 to 15 minutes (with the lid closed). Then use a brass bristle grill brush or grid scrubber to remove any baked-on food. This will also burn off some of the residue on your lava rocks or ceramic briquettes. If the lava rock contains a lot of residue, however, clean it by following your owner's manual instructions.

Peanut Sauced Chicken Satay Kabobs

4 **large boneless, skinless chicken breast halves (1 pound total)**
¼ **cup soy sauce**
2 **tablespoons cooking oil**
2 **tablespoons lemon juice**
1 **teaspoon curry powder**

1 **teaspoon toasted sesame oil**
¼ **teaspoon ground coriander**
1 **clove garlic, minced**
4 **to 5 tablespoons hot water**
¼ **cup peanut butter**
½ **teaspoon grated gingerroot**
⅛ **teaspoon crushed red pepper**

This Indonesian favorite teams strips of chicken threaded on skewers and a spicy peanut sauce. It's often served as an appetizer, too.

1 Rinse chicken; pat dry. Cut chicken breasts lengthwise into 1-inch-wide strips. Place chicken strips in a plastic bag set in a deep bowl. For marinade, combine soy sauce, cooking oil, lemon juice, curry powder, sesame oil, coriander, and garlic; pour over chicken. Close bag. Marinate in refrigerator for 1 to 2 hours, turning occasionally.

2 Meanwhile, for peanut sauce, in a small bowl gradually stir hot water into peanut butter till smooth and of a sauce-like consistency. Stir in gingerroot and red pepper. Set sauce aside.

3 Drain chicken, reserving marinade. On 8 long metal skewers, loosely thread chicken strips accordion-style. Preheat gas grill. Adjust heat for direct cooking. Place kabobs on grill rack over medium heat. Cover and grill kabobs for 5 to 6 minutes or till chicken is tender and no longer pink, brushing occasionally with reserved marinade and turning once halfway through.

4 Serve chicken strips with peanut sauce. Makes 4 servings.

Indirect Grilling: Preheat gas grill. Adjust heat for indirect cooking. Place kabobs on grill rack over medium heat. Cover and grill kabobs for 7 to 8 minutes or till chicken is tender and no longer pink, brushing occasionally with reserved marinade and turning once halfway through. Continue as directed above.

Per serving: 300 calories, 27 g protein, 6 g carbohydrate, 19 g total fat (4 g saturated), 59 mg cholesterol, 1,160 mg sodium, 345 mg potassium

Chicken and Beef Kabobs

The lemon adds a tang, the pepper lends a slight bite, and the baby carrots and summer squash contribute lots of color to these kabobs.

2 large boneless, skinless
  chicken breast halves
  (8 ounces total)
8 ounces boneless beef sirloin
  steak, cut 1 inch thick
1 tablespoon finely shredded
  lemon peel
⅓ cup lemon juice

¼ cup cooking oil
1 tablespoon brown sugar
1 teaspoon coarsely cracked
  pepper
¼ teaspoon salt
½ pound baby carrots
8 to 12 yellow sunburst or
  pattypan squash

1 Rinse chicken; pat dry. Trim fat from beef. Cut chicken and beef into 1-inch pieces. Place chicken and beef in a plastic bag set in a deep bowl.

2 For marinade, combine lemon peel, lemon juice, oil, brown sugar, pepper, and salt; pour over chicken and beef. Close bag. Marinate in refrigerator for 1 to 2 hours, turning occasionally.

3 Meanwhile, trim carrots, leaving ½ to 1 inch of stems; scrub but do not peel. In a medium saucepan cook carrots and squash, covered, in a small amount of boiling water for 3 minutes. Drain; cut any large squash in half.

4 Drain chicken and beef, reserving marinade. On 8 long metal skewers, alternately thread chicken, beef, and vegetables, leaving about ¼ inch between pieces.

5 Preheat gas grill. Adjust heat for direct cooking. Place kabobs on grill rack over medium heat. Cover and grill for 12 to 14 minutes or till chicken is tender and no longer pink, brushing occasionally with reserved marinade and turning kabobs once halfway through. Makes 4 servings.

Indirect Grilling: Preheat gas grill. Adjust heat for indirect cooking. Place kabobs on grill rack over medium heat. Cover and grill for 16 to 18 minutes or till chicken is tender and no longer pink, brushing occasionally with reserved marinade and turning kabobs once halfway through.

Per serving: 338 calories, 25 g protein, 13 g carbohydrate, 21 g total fat (5 g saturated), 68 mg cholesterol, 205 mg sodium, 509 mg potassium

Chicken-Vegetable Kabobs

4 large boneless, skinless
chicken breast halves
(1 pound total)
¼ cup lemon juice
2 tablespoons honey
2 tablespoons olive oil or
cooking oil
1 tablespoon snipped fresh
parsley
1 tablespoon snipped fresh
basil or 1 teaspoon dried
basil, crushed

1 tablespoon snipped fresh
oregano or 1 teaspoon
dried oregano, crushed
2 cloves garlic, minced
8 tiny whole new potatoes,
halved
2 cups broccoli flowerets
¼ teaspoon lemon-pepper
seasoning

New potatoes and broccoli flowerets make these tasty kabobs a little bit different.

1 Rinse chicken; pat dry. Cut chicken into 1-inch pieces. Place chicken in a plastic bag set in a shallow dish. For marinade, combine lemon juice, honey, oil, parsley, basil, oregano, and garlic; pour over chicken. Close bag. Marinate in refrigerator for 2 to 4 hours, turning occasionally.

2 Meanwhile, scrub new potatoes. In a medium saucepan cook potatoes, covered, in a small amount of boiling water for 8 minutes. Add broccoli and cook for 1 to 2 minutes more or till crisp-tender. Drain.

3 Drain chicken, reserving marinade. On 8 long metal skewers, alternately thread chicken, potatoes, and broccoli, leaving about ¼ inch between the pieces. Sprinkle kabobs with lemon-pepper seasoning.

4 Preheat gas grill. Adjust heat for direct cooking. Place kabobs on grill rack over medium heat. Cover and grill for 12 to 14 minutes or till chicken is tender and no longer pink, brushing with reserved marinade and turning kabobs once halfway through. Makes 4 servings.

Indirect Grilling: Preheat gas grill. Adjust heat for indirect cooking. Place kabobs on grill rack over medium heat. Cover and grill for 16 to 18 minutes or till chicken is tender and no longer pink, brushing with reserved marinade and turning kabobs once halfway through.

Per serving: 268 calories, 25 g protein, 27 g carbohydrate, 7 g total fat (1 g saturated), 59 mg cholesterol, 143 mg sodium, 727 mg potassium

Dollop It with Butter

Give ordinary grilled entrées extra zip by dressing them up with one of these flavored spreads. They aren't complicated—just a simple mix of a few tasty ingredients. You'll find them delicious and easy to use.

In This Chapter:

Tenderloins with Blue Cheese Butter

¼ cup margarine or butter,
  softened
½ teaspoon lemon juice
⅛ teaspoon pepper

¼ cup crumbled blue cheese
8 slices bacon
4 10-ounce beef tenderloin or
  top loin steaks, cut 1 inch
  thick

The bold flavor of this tangy butter, melting over a juicy, sizzling steak, will delight your guests.

1 For blue cheese butter, in a small mixing bowl stir together margarine or butter, lemon juice, and pepper. Fold in blue cheese and mix just till combined. Refrigerate till needed.

2 In a skillet cook bacon till almost done, but not crisp. Drain off fat. Pat bacon with paper towels to remove excess fat. Wrap bacon around steaks, securing with wooden toothpicks.

3 Preheat gas grill. Adjust heat for direct cooking. Place steaks on grill rack over medium heat. Cover and grill for 8 to 12 minutes for rare (140°) or 12 to 15 minutes for medium (160°). Serve steaks with a spoonful of blue cheese butter. Makes 4 servings.

Indirect Grilling: Preheat gas grill. Adjust heat for indirect cooking. Place steaks on grill rack over medium heat. Cover and grill for 16 to 20 minutes for rare (140°) or 20 to 24 minutes for medium (160°). Continue as directed above.

Per serving: 593 calories, 60 g protein, 0 g carbohydrate, 38 g total fat (13 g saturated), 177 mg cholesterol, 574 mg sodium, 889 mg potassium

Lamb Chops with Pesto Butter

So easy to prepare, so delicious to eat! Serve these marinated lamb chops at your next summer get-together.

8 lamb loin chops, cut 1 inch thick (about 2½ pounds total)
⅓ cup dry white wine
⅓ cup lemon juice
¼ cup finely chopped onion
3 tablespoons olive oil or cooking oil

1 tablespoon snipped fresh basil or 1 teaspoon dried basil, crushed
½ teaspoon salt
¼ teaspoon pepper
Pesto Butter

1 Trim fat from meat. Place chops in a plastic bag set in a deep bowl. For marinade, combine wine, lemon juice, onion, oil, basil, salt, and pepper; pour over lamb. Close bag. Marinate in refrigerator for 6 to 24 hours, turning occasionally.

2 Drain chops, reserving marinade. Preheat gas grill. Adjust heat for direct cooking. Place lamb chops on grill rack over medium heat. Cover and grill for 10 to 16 minutes or till desired doneness, brushing with reserved marinade and turning once halfway through.

3 Serve chops with a spoonful of Pesto Butter. Makes 4 servings.

Indirect Grilling: Preheat gas grill. Adjust heat for indirect cooking. Place lamb chops on grill rack over medium heat. Cover and grill for 16 to 20 minutes or till desired doneness, brushing with reserved marinade and turning once halfway through. Continue as directed above.

Pesto Butter: In a food processor bowl combine ½ cup firmly packed fresh *basil leaves*; ¼ cup grated *Parmesan cheese*; 2 tablespoons *pine nuts or walnuts*; 1 tablespoon *olive oil or cooking oil*; and 1 clove *garlic*, minced. Cover and process till a paste forms. Stir mixture into ¼ cup softened *margarine or butter*. Cover and refrigerate till needed.

Per serving: *538 calories, 40 g protein, 2 g carbohydrate, 40 g total fat (10 g saturated), 130 mg cholesterol, 483 mg sodium, 491 mg potassium*

Chicken with Tarragon-Citrus Butter

4 large boneless, skinless
   chicken breast halves
   (1 pound total)
½ teaspoon finely shredded
   orange peel
½ cup orange juice
¼ cup dry white wine
½ teaspoon finely shredded
   lemon peel
2 tablespoons lemon juice
1 tablespoon cooking oil

1 clove garlic, minced
¼ cup margarine or butter,
   softened
2 teaspoons snipped fresh
   tarragon or ½ teaspoon
   dried tarragon, crushed
½ teaspoon finely shredded
   orange peel
½ teaspoon finely shredded
   lemon peel
½ teaspoon orange juice or
   lemon juice

1 Rinse chicken; pat dry. Place in a plastic bag set in a shallow dish. For marinade, combine ½ teaspoon orange peel, the ½ cup orange juice, wine, ½ teaspoon lemon peel, lemon juice, oil, and garlic; pour over chicken. Close bag. Marinate in refrigerator for 2 to 4 hours, turning occasionally.

2 Meanwhile, for butter, in a small mixing bowl combine margarine or butter, tarragon, ½ teaspoon orange peel, ½ teaspoon lemon peel, and the ½ teaspoon orange juice or lemon juice. Cover and refrigerate.

3 Drain chicken, reserving marinade. Preheat gas grill. Adjust heat for direct cooking. Place chicken breasts on grill rack over medium heat. Cover and grill for 12 to 15 minutes or till chicken is tender and no longer pink, turning once and brushing occasionally with reserved marinade before turning. Serve chicken breast halves with a spoonful of butter. Makes 4 servings.

Indirect Grilling: Preheat gas grill. Adjust heat for indirect cooking. Place chicken breasts on a grill rack over medium heat. Cover and grill for 15 to 18 minutes or till chicken is tender and no longer pink, turning once and brushing occasionally with reserved marinade before turning. Continue as directed above.

Per serving: 281 calories, 22 g protein, 5 g carbohydrate, 18 g total fat (4 g saturated), 59 mg cholesterol, 189 mg sodium, 271 mg potassium

Salmon with Lemon Mayonnaise

1 1½-pound boneless, skinless fresh or frozen salmon fillet
½ cup mayonnaise or salad dressing
2 tablespoons snipped fresh chives
1 teaspoon finely shredded lemon peel
1 tablespoon lemon juice
1 tablespoon snipped fresh parsley
¼ teaspoon coarsely cracked pepper
2 tablespoons lemon juice
1½ teaspoons olive oil or cooking oil
½ teaspoon Worcestershire sauce
1 teaspoon snipped fresh rosemary or ¼ teaspoon dried rosemary, crushed

1 Thaw salmon, if frozen. For mayonnaise mixture, in a small mixing bowl stir together mayonnaise or salad dressing, chives, lemon peel, the 1 tablespoon lemon juice, parsley, and pepper. Cover and refrigerate. In a small mixing bowl combine the 2 tablespoons lemon juice, olive oil, Worcestershire sauce, and rosemary; set aside.

2 Place salmon in a greased grill basket. (Or, cut several slits in a piece of heavy foil large enough to hold fish. Grease foil; place fish on foil.) Turn under the thin ends of the fillet to make an even thickness. Measure thickness of fillet. Close basket.

3 Preheat gas grill. Adjust heat for direct cooking. Place grill basket (or foil) on grill rack over medium heat. Cover and grill for 4 to 6 minutes per ½ inch thickness of fish or just till fish begins to flake easily, brushing often with lemon juice mixture and turning once halfway through.

4 Serve fillet with a spoonful of mayonnaise mixture. Makes 6 servings.

Indirect Grilling: Cut several slits in a piece of heavy foil large enough to hold fish. Grease foil; place fish on foil. Turn under thin ends to make an even thickness. Preheat gas grill. Adjust heat for indirect cooking. Place foil with fish on grill rack over medium heat. Cover and grill for 14 to 16 minutes or just till fish begins to flake easily, brushing twice with lemon juice mixture. Continue as directed above.

Per serving: 249 calories, 17 g protein, 2 g carbohydrate, 20 g total fat (3 g saturated), 31 mg cholesterol, 179 mg sodium, 181 mg potassium

Fish Steaks with Cilantro-Lime Butter

4 6-ounce fresh or frozen
   halibut, swordfish, shark, or
   salmon steaks, cut
   1 inch thick
¼ cup margarine or butter,
   softened

1 tablespoon snipped fresh
   cilantro
1 teaspoon finely chopped
   jalapeño pepper
1 teaspoon finely shredded
   lime peel
½ teaspoon lime juice
1 tablespoon olive oil

Try this tasty, southwestern-flavored butter on boneless chicken-breasts or pork chops, too.

1 Thaw fish, if frozen. For butter, in a small mixing bowl combine margarine or butter, cilantro, jalapeño pepper, lime peel, and lime juice. Set aside.

2 Brush grill rack lightly with oil. Preheat gas grill. Adjust heat for direct cooking. Brush both sides of fish steaks with olive oil. Place fish steaks on grill rack over medium heat. Cover and grill for 8 to 12 minutes or just till fish begins to flake easily, brushing with olive oil and turning once halfway through. Serve with butter. Makes 4 servings.

Indirect Grilling: Preheat gas grill. Adjust heat for indirect cooking. Brush both sides of fish steaks with olive oil. Place fish steaks on grill rack over medium heat. Cover and grill for 8 to 12 minutes or just till fish begins to flake easily, brushing with olive oil and turning once halfway through. Continue as directed above.

Per serving: *318 calories, 36 g protein, 0 g carbohydrate, 19 g total fat (3 g saturated), 55 mg cholesterol, 226 mg sodium, 776 mg potassium*

Stuff It with Stuff

What do a chop, a chicken breast, and a roast have in common? You can stuff them all with no-fuss fillings of rice, fruit, vegetables, and even seafood, for some of the most scrumptious entrées your gas grill has to offer.

In This Chapter:

Stuffed Flank Steak Oriental

1 1½-pound beef flank steak,
  cut about 1 inch thick
¼ cup soy sauce
¼ cup orange juice
2 tablespoons molasses
1 tablespoon cooking oil
1 teaspoon dry mustard
½ teaspoon ground ginger

2 cloves garlic, minced
⅔ cup beef broth
⅓ cup shredded carrot
⅓ cup long grain rice
⅓ cup chopped water
  chestnuts
¼ cup thinly sliced green onion

1 To cut a pocket in flank steak, insert the tip of a long-bladed knife horizontally into the short end of the steak. Slit a pocket the full width and length of the steak, cutting to but not through edges, so steak remains connected on three sides. Place in a plastic bag set in a shallow dish.

2 For marinade, combine soy sauce, orange juice, molasses, oil, mustard, ginger, and garlic; pour over steak. Close bag. Marinate in refrigerator for 6 to 24 hours, turning occasionally.

3 For stuffing, in a small saucepan combine beef broth, carrot, rice, and water chestnuts. Bring to boiling. Reduce heat and simmer, covered, about 15 minutes or till rice is tender and liquid is absorbed. Remove from heat. Drain flank steak, reserving marinade. Bring 3 tablespoons reserved marinade to boiling; stir into stuffing. Stir in green onion. Spoon hot stuffing into pocket in meat. Secure with small skewers or wooden toothpicks.

4 Preheat gas grill. Adjust heat for direct cooking. Place steak on grill rack over medium heat. Cover and grill for 12 to 14 minutes or till desired doneness, brushing with remaining reserved marinade and turning once halfway through.

5 To serve, slice meat across the grain into ½-inch-thick slices. Makes 4 servings.

Per serving: 265 calories, 23 g protein, 13 g carbohydrate, 13 g total fat (4 g saturated), 53 mg cholesterol, 501 mg sodium, 436 mg potassium

Beef Rolls Italiano

Sprinkle these sausage-and-spinach stuffed beef rolls with some freshly grated Parmesan cheese before serving.

- 1 pound boneless beef top round steak, cut ½ inch thick
- 2 tablespoons olive oil or cooking oil
- 2 tablespoons red wine vinegar
- 1 tablespoon snipped fresh thyme or 1 teaspoon dried thyme, crushed
- 1 tablespoon snipped fresh oregano or 1 teaspoon dried oregano, crushed

- ¼ teaspoon sugar
- ¼ teaspoon pepper
  Dash bottled hot pepper sauce
- ¼ pound bulk Italian sausage
- ¼ cup chopped onion
- 1 cup chopped fresh spinach
- 1 14½-ounce can pasta-style tomatoes

1 Trim fat from meat. Cut round steak into 4 pieces. Place each piece of beef between 2 pieces of plastic wrap. Working from the center to the edges, pound lightly with the flat side of a meat mallet to form a rectangle (about ⅛ inch thick). Remove and discard plastic wrap. Place meat in a plastic bag set in a shallow dish. For marinade, combine oil, vinegar, thyme, oregano, sugar, pepper, and hot pepper sauce; pour over meat. Close bag. Marinate in refrigerator for 4 to 24 hours, turning occasionally.

2 Meanwhile, for filling, in a skillet cook sausage and onion till brown; drain off fat. Stir spinach into sausage mixture till wilted; set filling aside. Drain steak, reserving marinade. Place ¼ of the filling at one end of each piece of beef. Fold bottom edge over filling and fold in sides. Roll beef up jelly-roll style. Secure with small metal skewers or wooden toothpicks.

3 Preheat gas grill. Adjust heat for indirect cooking. Place beef rolls on grill rack over medium heat. Cover and grill 20 to 25 minutes or till beef is tender, turning once halfway through.

4 Meanwhile, for sauce, in a medium saucepan bring the undrained tomatoes to boiling. Reduce heat and simmer, uncovered, about 5 minutes or till slightly thickened. To serve, remove skewers or toothpicks. Serve beef rolls with sauce. Makes 4 servings.

Per serving: *301 calories, 33 g protein, 9 g carbohydrate, 14 g total fat (4 g saturated), 88 mg cholesterol, 616 mg sodium, 847 mg potassium*

Apple-Jalapeño Chops

½ cup shredded Monterey Jack
    cheese with jalapeño
    peppers
¼ cup finely chopped apple
1 tablespoon chopped almonds
1 tablespoon snipped fresh
    cilantro

4 pork loin or rib chops, cut
    1¼ inches thick
    (about 2¼ pounds total)
½ cup apple jelly
1 jalapeño pepper, seeded and
    chopped
2 tablespoons apple juice or
    water
1½ teaspoons cornstarch

The sweetness of the apple glaze complements the hotness of the jalapeño peppers.

1 For stuffing, in a small bowl toss together the shredded cheese, chopped apple, almonds, and cilantro. Set aside. Trim fat from meat. Make a pocket in each chop by cutting horizontally into the chop from the fat side almost to the bone. Spoon about ¼ cup of the stuffing into each pocket. If necessary, securely fasten the opening with toothpicks.

2 For glaze, in a small saucepan combine jelly and jalapeño pepper. Cook and stir over low heat till jelly melts. Combine apple juice or water and cornstarch; stir into jelly mixture. Cook and stir till thickened and bubbly. Cook and stir 2 minutes more.

3 Preheat gas grill. Adjust heat for indirect cooking. Place chops on grill rack over medium heat. Cover and grill for 40 to 50 minutes or till juices run clear, turning once halfway through and brushing with glaze after 25 minutes. Makes 4 servings.

Per serving: *409 calories, 31 g protein, 30 g carbohydrate, 18 g total fat (7 g saturated), 99 mg cholesterol, 149 mg sodium, 431 mg potassium*

Rice and Apricot-Stuffed Pork Chops

To get the ½ cup of cooked wild rice needed for this tasty stuffing, start with ¼ cup uncooked wild rice and ½ cup water. Cook according to package directions.

2 tablespoons finely chopped celery
2 tablespoons thinly sliced green onion
1 tablespoon margarine or butter
½ cup cooked wild rice
3 tablespoons finely snipped dried apricots

¼ teaspoon salt
⅛ teaspoon pepper
4 pork loin or rib chops, cut 1¼ inches thick (about 2¼ pounds total)
¼ cup apricot preserves
1 tablespoon dry white wine or apple juice
⅛ teaspoon ground cinnamon

1 For stuffing, in a small saucepan cook celery and green onion in margarine or butter till tender. Stir in rice, apricots, salt, and pepper. Set aside.

2 Trim fat from meat. Make a pocket in each chop by cutting horizontally into the chop from the fat side almost to the bone. Spoon about 3 tablespoons of the stuffing into each pocket. If necessary, securely fasten the opening with wooden toothpicks.

3 For glaze, snip any large pieces of apricot in preserves. Combine apricot preserves, wine or apple juice, and cinnamon; set aside.

4 Preheat gas grill. Adjust heat for indirect cooking. Place chops on grill rack over medium heat. Cover and grill about 35 minutes or till juices run clear, turning once halfway through and brushing with glaze after 25 minutes. Makes 4 servings.

Per serving: 351 calories, 28 g protein, 23 g carbohydrate, 15 g total fat (5 g saturated), 86 mg cholesterol, 240 mg sodium, 504 mg potassium

Pork Roast with Vegetable Stuffing

¼ cup thinly sliced green onion
¼ cup finely chopped sweet red pepper
¼ cup shredded carrot
1 tablespoon margarine or butter

¾ cup corn bread stuffing mix
½ cup whole kernel corn
¼ teaspoon salt
¼ teaspoon pepper
1 3-pound pork loin center rib roast, backbone loosened

At 160°, the pork roast will still be slightly pink in the center, but the juices should run clear.

1 For stuffing, in a small saucepan cook green onion, sweet red pepper, and carrot in margarine or butter till tender but not brown. Stir in stuffing mix, corn, salt, and pepper.

2 Trim fat from meat. Place roast rib side down. Cut pockets in roast from meaty side between the rib bones. Spoon stuffing into pockets. Insert a meat thermometer near center of roast not touching bone.

3 Preheat gas grill. Adjust heat for indirect cooking. Place meat on a rack in a roasting pan on the grill rack over medium heat. Cover and grill for 1½ to 2 hours or till meat thermometer registers 160°.

4 To serve, slice lengthwise along the backbone to separate the meat from the bone. Slice crosswise between pockets. Makes 4 servings.

Per serving: 297 calories, 23 g protein, 21 g carbohydrate, 13 g total fat (4 g saturated), 64 mg cholesterol, 649 mg sodium, 396 mg potassium

Cranberry and Apple Pork Tenderloins

When dried cranberries or cherries are not available, mixed dried fruit bits make a great substitute.

2 12-ounce pork tenderloins
⅔ cup apple juice
1 teaspoon instant chicken bouillon granules
¼ cup dried cranberries or cherries
¼ cup snipped dried apples
2 tablespoons finely chopped onion

1 tablespoon margarine or butter
⅛ teaspoon ground cinnamon
⅛ teaspoon pepper
2 cups dry whole wheat bread cubes
1 tablespoon cooking oil

1 Split both tenderloins lengthwise, cutting to but not through the opposite side. Spread meat open. Overlap one long side of each tenderloin about 2 inches. Place pork between 2 pieces of plastic wrap. Working from the center to the edges, pound lightly with the flat side of a meat mallet to form a 12 x 10-inch rectangle, about ⅛- to ¼-inch thick. Remove plastic wrap.

2 For stuffing, bring apple juice to boiling; stir in bouillon granules till dissolved. Pour hot apple juice mixture over dried cranberries or cherries and apples. Let stand 5 minutes.

3 Meanwhile, in a small saucepan cook onion in margarine or butter till tender but not brown. Remove from heat and stir in cinnamon and pepper. Place bread cubes in a large mixing bowl and add onion mixture and cranberry-apple mixture; toss lightly to moisten.

4 Spoon stuffing over meat to within 1 inch of edge of meat. Roll up jelly-roll style, beginning at one of the short sides. Tie with string at 1-inch intervals. Brush meat with a little cooking oil.

5 Preheat gas grill. Adjust heat for indirect cooking. Place meat on a rack in a roasting pan on the grill rack over medium heat. Cover and grill about 1½ hours or till juices run clear, occasionally brushing meat with cooking oil. Makes 6 servings.

Per serving: 244 calories, 26 g protein, 14 g carbohydrate, 9 g total fat (2 g saturated), 81 mg cholesterol, 289 mg sodium, 546 mg potassium

Corn Bread and Ham-Stuffed Chicken

2 whole medium chicken
   breasts (about 1½ pounds
   total)
2 tablespoons thinly sliced
   green onion
2 tablespoons finely chopped
   celery
1 tablespoon margarine or
   butter

1½ cups corn bread stuffing mix
¼ cup diced fully cooked ham
¼ cup water
1 tablespoon snipped fresh
   parsley
⅛ teaspoon ground sage
1 tablespoon cooking oil

1 Rinse chicken; pat dry. Bone and halve chicken breasts, leaving skin attached. Beginning on one of the long sides, gently loosen the skin from the chicken breast half, leaving skin attached at the other side.

2 For stuffing, in a small saucepan cook green onion and celery in margarine or butter till tender. Stir in stuffing mix, ham, water, parsley, and sage. Stuff about ⅓ cup of the stuffing mixture between the skin and flesh of each breast half. Brush chicken with oil.

3 Preheat gas grill. Adjust heat for indirect cooking. Place chicken breasts, skin side up, on a rack in a roasting pan on the grill rack over medium heat. Cover and grill for 40 to 50 minutes or till chicken is tender and no longer pink. Makes 4 servings.

Per serving: 375 calories, 35 g protein, 25 g carbohydrate, 14 g total fat (3 g saturated), 88 mg cholesterol, 699 mg sodium, 302 mg potassium

Italian-Stuffed Chicken Breasts

A wonderful blend of ricotta, mozzarella, and Parmesan cheeses accents these grilled chicken breasts.

2 whole medium chicken breasts (about 1½ pounds total)
½ cup ricotta cheese
½ cup shredded mozzarella cheese
¼ cup grated Parmesan or Romano cheese
2 tablespoons snipped fresh parsley

2 teaspoons snipped fresh basil or ½ teaspoon dried basil, crushed
1 teaspoon snipped fresh oregano or ¼ teaspoon dried oregano, crushed
1 clove garlic, minced
1 teaspoon olive oil or cooking oil
Paprika

1 Rinse chicken; pat dry. Bone and halve chicken breasts, leaving skin attached. Beginning on one of the long sides, gently loosen the skin from the chicken breast half, leaving skin attached at the other side.

2 For stuffing, combine ricotta cheese, mozzarella cheese, Parmesan or Romano cheese, parsley, basil, oregano, and garlic. Stuff about ⅓ cup of the stuffing mixture between the skin and flesh of each breast half. Brush chicken with oil. Sprinkle with paprika.

3 Preheat gas grill. Adjust heat for indirect cooking. Place chicken breast, skin side up, on a rack in a roasting pan on the grill rack over medium heat. Cover and grill for 50 to 60 minutes or till chicken is tender and no longer pink. Makes 4 servings.

Per serving: 301 calories, 42 g protein, 3 g carbohydrate, 12 g total fat (6 g saturated), 112 mg cholesterol, 302 mg sodium, 336 mg potassium

Prosciutto-and-Basil-Stuffed Chicken

4 large boneless, skinless
  chicken breast halves
  (1 pound total)
1 tablespoon coarse-grain
  brown mustard
2 to 3 ounces thinly sliced
  prosciutto or very thinly
  sliced ham

12 to 16 fresh basil leaves,
  stems removed
3 tablespoons olive oil
¼ teaspoon pepper
⅛ teaspoon garlic powder

Whole fresh basil leaves and thin slices of prosciutto are rolled up inside these succulent chicken breasts.

1 Rinse chicken; pat dry. Place each breast half between 2 pieces of plastic wrap. Working from the center to the edges, pound lightly with the flat side of a meat mallet to ⅛-inch thickness. Remove plastic wrap.

2 Spread a thin layer of mustard over each chicken breast half. Top each breast half with a slice of prosciutto or ham and 3 or 4 basil leaves. Fold in sides of each chicken breast; roll up jelly-roll style. Fasten with wooden toothpicks.

3 For sauce, in a small mixing bowl combine the olive oil, pepper, and garlic powder.

4 Preheat gas grill. Adjust heat for direct cooking. Place chicken on grill rack over medium heat. Cover and grill for 15 to 18 minutes or till the chicken is tender and no longer pink, turning once halfway through and brushing occasionally with sauce the last 10 minutes. Makes 4 servings.

Indirect Grilling: Preheat gas grill. Adjust heat for indirect cooking. Place chicken on grill rack over medium heat. Cover and grill about 20 minutes or till chicken is tender and no longer pink, turning once halfway through and brushing occasionally with sauce the last 10 minutes.

Per serving: 260 calories, 25 g protein, 0 g carbohydrate, 17 g total fat (2 g saturated), 59 mg cholesterol, 355 mg sodium, 192 mg potassium

Grilled Trout with Fruit Stuffing

4 8- to 10-ounce fresh or
frozen dressed trout
⅓ cup chopped onion
1 tablespoon margarine or
butter
1½ cups herb-seasoned
stuffing mix

½ cup mixed dried fruit bits
¼ teaspoon salt
⅛ teaspoon ground allspice
4 to 5 tablespoons apple juice
or water
1 tablespoon margarine or
butter, melted

1 Thaw fish, if frozen. For stuffing, in a medium saucepan cook onion in 1 tablespoon margarine or butter till tender but not brown. Stir in stuffing mix, fruit bits, salt, and allspice. Toss lightly till well mixed. Add apple juice or water as necessary to moisten, tossing gently to mix.

2 Spoon ¼ of the stuffing into each fish cavity. Skewer cavities closed with wooden toothpicks. Cut several slits in a piece of heavy foil large enough to hold fish. Grease foil and place fish on it. Drizzle fish with 1 tablespoon melted margarine or butter.

3 Preheat gas grill. Adjust heat for indirect cooking. Place foil with fish on the grill rack over medium heat. Cover and grill for 15 to 20 minutes or just till fish begins to flake easily.

4 Remove toothpicks. Makes 4 servings.

Per serving: 436 calories, 39 g protein, 40 g carbohydrate, 13 g total fat (2 g saturated), 97 mg cholesterol, 686 mg sodium, 1,016 mg potassium

Crab-Stuffed Lobster Tails

4 medium fresh or frozen rock
    lobster tails (about
    5 ounces each)
3 tablespoons sliced green
    onion
1 tablespoon margarine or
    butter
1½ teaspoons all-purpose flour
1 teaspoon snipped fresh dill
    or ¼ teaspoon dried
    dillweed

¼ cup half-and-half, light
    cream, or milk
1 6-ounce can crabmeat,
    drained, flaked, and
    cartilage removed
1 tablespoon dry white wine
2 tablespoons margarine or
    butter, melted

*Two seafood
delicacies
combine to make
one very rich
grilled entrée.*

1 Thaw lobster, if frozen. Rinse lobster; pat dry. Butterfly tails by using
kitchen shears or a sharp knife to cut lengthwise through centers of
hard top shells and meat. Cut to, but not through, bottom shells. Press
shell halves of tails apart with your fingers.

2 For stuffing, in a small saucepan cook green onion in the 1 tablespoon
margarine or butter till tender but not brown. Stir in flour and dill. Add
half-and-half, light cream, or milk all at once. Cook and stir till thickened
and bubbly. Cook and stir 2 minutes more. Remove from heat. Gently
stir in the crabmeat and wine.

3 Carefully spoon crabmeat stuffing onto lobster meat. Drizzle stuffed
tails with the 2 tablespoons margarine or butter.

4 Preheat gas grill. Adjust heat for indirect cooking. Place lobster tails,
filled side down, on grill rack over medium heat. Cover and grill about
25 minutes or till lobster meat turns opaque and stuffing is heated
through. Makes 4 servings.

*Per serving: 233 calories, 28 g protein, 3 g carbohydrate, 11 g total fat
(3 g saturated), 108 mg cholesterol, 593 mg sodium, 511 mg potassium*

Serve It on the Side

The "fixins" in this chapter are the quick-and-easy kind of extras that make your grilled meal extraordinary. The appetizers, side dishes, breads, and desserts in this tasty assortment of recipes are easy to grill right alongside your main dish.

In This Chapter:

New Potatoes with Roasted Garlic

2 pounds tiny new potatoes, sliced	**1 tablespoon olive oil or cooking oil**
4 large cloves garlic	**1 tablespoon white wine vinegar**
1 tablespoon olive oil or cooking oil	**2 teaspoons Dijon-style mustard**
¼ teaspoon salt	**¼ teaspoon pepper**
4 sprigs fresh rosemary	

Shop your local Farmer's Market for new potatoes and fresh herbs.

1 Tear off a 36 x 18-inch piece of heavy foil. Fold in half to make a double thickness of foil that measures 18 x 18 inches.

2 In a large mixing bowl combine sliced potatoes, unpeeled garlic cloves, 1 tablespoon olive oil, and salt; toss gently. Place potato mixture in the center of the foil. Top with rosemary sprigs. Bring up the two opposite edges of the foil and seal with a double fold. Fold remaining ends to completely enclose the potato mixture, leaving space for steam to build.

3 Preheat gas grill. Adjust heat for direct cooking. Place foil packet on grill rack over medium heat. Cover and grill about 35 minutes or till potatoes are tender. Discard rosemary sprigs.

4 Meanwhile, in a screw-top jar combine 1 tablespoon olive oil, vinegar, mustard, and pepper. Squeeze the paste from the grilled garlic cloves into screw-top jar. Cover; shake well. Pour garlic mixture over grilled potatoes; toss gently to coat. Makes 4 servings.

Per serving: 290 calories, 6 g protein, 52 g carbohydrate, 7 g total fat (1 g saturated), 0 mg cholesterol, 245 mg sodium, 1,010 mg potassium

Vegetables with Dill Butter

If you grow your own fresh herbs, you can easily make your own variations of this savory butter. Try oregano, basil, rosemary, or thyme.

2 tablespoons margarine or butter
4 teaspoons snipped fresh dill or 1 teaspoon dried dillweed
¼ teaspoon salt
¼ teaspoon pepper
4 medium carrots, sliced (2 cups)

2 cups cubed potatoes
1 small yellow summer squash or zucchini, halved lengthwise and cut into ½-inch-thick slices (1 cup)
Nonstick spray coating
4 slices bacon, crisp-cooked, drained, and crumbled

1 In a small saucepan melt margarine or butter. Stir in dill, salt, and pepper. Set aside.

2 In a medium mixing bowl toss together carrots, potatoes, and summer squash or zucchini.

3 Tear off a 36 x 18-inch piece of heavy foil. Fold in half to make a double thickness of foil that measures 18 x 18 inches. Spray center of foil with nonstick spray coating. Place vegetables in center of foil. Drizzle butter mixture over vegetables. Top with crumbled bacon. Bring up two opposite edges of foil and seal with a double fold. Fold remaining ends to completely enclose the vegetables, leaving space for steam to build.

4 Preheat gas grill. Adjust heat for direct cooking. Place foil packet on grill rack over medium heat. Cover and grill about 30 minutes or till vegetables are tender. Makes 4 to 5 servings.

Per serving: 197 calories, 5 g protein, 25 g carbohydrate, 9 g total fat (2 g saturated), 5 mg cholesterol, 353 mg sodium, 567 mg potassium

Grilled Ratatouille

1 **small eggplant, cut into ¾-inch cubes (5 cups)**
1 **small zucchini or yellow summer squash, sliced ½ inch thick (1 cup)**
2 **medium tomatoes, peeled and chopped (1½ cups)**
1 **small green pepper, cut into bite-size strips (1 cup)**
½ **cup chopped onion**
2 **tablespoons dry white wine or water**
1 **tablespoon olive oil or cooking oil**
2 **cloves garlic, minced**
1 **tablespoon snipped fresh basil or 1 teaspoon dried basil, crushed**
½ **teaspoon lemon-pepper seasoning**
¼ **cup finely shredded Parmesan cheese**

This Mediterranean vegetable dish steams inside a foil packet on the grill.

1 In a large mixing bowl combine eggplant, zucchini or summer squash, tomatoes, green pepper, and onion.

2 In a small mixing bowl combine wine or water, oil, garlic, basil, and lemon-pepper seasoning. Set aside.

3 Tear off a 36 x 18-inch piece of heavy foil. Fold in half to make a double thickness of foil that measures 18 x 18 inches. Place vegetables in center of foil. Drizzle oil mixture over vegetables. Bring up two opposite edges of foil and seal with a double fold. Fold remaining ends to completely enclose the vegetables, leaving space for steam to build.

4 Preheat gas grill. Adjust heat for direct cooking. Place foil packet on grill rack over medium heat. Cover and grill about 40 minutes or till vegetables are very tender. Sprinkle with Parmesan cheese. Serve with a slotted spoon. Makes 4 servings.

Per serving: 88 calories, 2 g protein, 12 g carbohydrate, 4 g total fat (1 g saturated), 0 mg cholesterol, 149 mg sodium, 454 mg potassium

Peppers Stuffed with Goat Cheese

These delicious peppers can be cut into strips and served as appetizers, if you like.

2 medium sweet red or yellow peppers
1 ounce soft goat cheese (chevre)
¼ cup shredded Monterey Jack cheese

1 tablespoon snipped fresh chives
1 tablespoon snipped fresh basil or 1 teaspoon dried basil, crushed

1 Halve peppers lengthwise, removing stem ends, seeds, and membranes. Cook peppers in a small amount of boiling water for 2 minutes. Drain peppers, cut side down, on paper towels. Set peppers aside.

2 For cheese mixture, in a small mixing bowl combine goat cheese, Monterey Jack cheese, chives, and basil; mix well. Place about 2 table-spoons of the cheese mixture in each pepper half.

3 Tear off a 24 x 18-inch piece of heavy foil. Fold in half to make a double thickness of foil that measures 12 x 18 inches. Place peppers in center of foil. Bring up two opposite edges of foil and seal with a double fold. Fold remaining ends to completely enclose the peppers, leaving space for steam to build.

4 Preheat gas grill. Adjust heat for direct cooking. Place foil packet on grill rack over medium to medium-high heat. Cover and grill for 5 to 6 minutes or till peppers are crisp-tender and cheese melts. Makes 4 servings.

Per serving: 60 calories, 3 g protein, 3 g carbohydrate, 4 g total fat (2 g saturated), 13 mg cholesterol, 80 mg sodium, 75 mg potassium

Vegetable-Horseradish Casserole

2 cups broccoli flowerets
1½ cups cauliflower flowerets
1½ cups thinly sliced carrots
½ cup mayonnaise or salad
    dressing
2 tablespoons finely chopped
    onion
4 teaspoons prepared
    horseradish

¼ teaspoon lemon-pepper
    seasoning
¼ cup seasoned fine dry bread
    crumbs
1 tablespoon margarine or
    butter, melted

1 In a large mixing bowl combine broccoli, cauliflower, and carrots. For horseradish mixture, in a small mixing bowl combine mayonnaise or salad dressing, onion, horseradish, and lemon-pepper seasoning. Stir horseradish mixture into vegetables.

2 Tear off a 36 x 18-inch piece of heavy foil. Fold in half to make a double thickness of foil that measures 18 x 18 inches. Spray center of foil with nonstick spray coating. Place vegetable mixture in center of foil.

3 Combine bread crumbs and margarine or butter; sprinkle over the vegetables.

4 Bring up two opposite edges of foil and seal with a double fold. Fold remaining ends to completely enclose the vegetables, leaving space for steam to build.

5 Preheat gas grill. Adjust heat for direct cooking. Place foil packet on grill rack over medium heat. Cover and grill for 30 minutes or till vegetables are tender. Makes 6 servings.

Per serving: 204 calories, 3 g protein, 12 g carbohydrate, 17 g total fat (3 g saturated), 11 mg cholesterol, 274 mg sodium, 334 mg potassium

Oriental Green Beans

Serve this easy side dish with steaks or chops.

2 tablespoons soy sauce
1 tablespoon water
⅛ teaspoon ground ginger
⅛ teaspoon pepper

2 cups bias-sliced green beans
½ cup sliced water chestnuts
2 tablespoons sliced or
   slivered almonds, toasted

1 In a small mixing bowl stir together soy sauce, water, salt, ginger, and pepper; set aside.

2 Tear off a 24 x 18-inch piece of heavy foil. Fold in half to make a double thickness of foil that measures 12 x 18 inches. Place green beans and water chestnuts in center of foil. Drizzle soy sauce mixture over green bean mixture. Bring up two opposite edges of foil and seal with a double fold. Fold remaining ends to completely enclose the vegetables, leaving space for steam to build.

3 Preheat gas grill. Adjust heat for direct cooking. Place foil packet on grill rack over medium to medium-high heat. Cover and grill for 20 to 25 minutes or till beans are crisp-tender.

4 Sprinkle beans with almonds. Makes 4 servings.

Per serving: *52 calories, 3 g protein, 8 g carbohydrate, 2 g total fat (0 g saturated), 0 mg cholesterol, 518 mg sodium, 228 mg potassium*

Grilled Mixed Veggies

**1½ pounds tiny new potatoes,
eggplant, zucchini or
yellow summer squash,
and/or sweet peppers**
**3 tablespoons olive oil or
cooking oil**
**1 tablespoon snipped fresh
basil or 1 teaspoon dried
basil, crushed**

**1 tablespoon snipped fresh
thyme or 1 teaspoon dried
thyme, crushed**
½ teaspoon onion powder
¼ teaspoon pepper
⅛ teaspoon dry mustard
⅛ teaspoon paprika
1 clove garlic, minced

*Take your pick of
vegetables from
new potatoes,
eggplant, summer
squash, or sweet
peppers.*

1 If using tiny new potatoes, halve potatoes and cook, covered, in a small
amount of boiling water about 10 minutes or till almost tender. Drain.

2 Meanwhile, if using eggplant or zucchini, cut off both ends. (Peel eggplant, if desired.) Cut eggplant crosswise into 1-inch-thick slices; quarter
zucchini lengthwise. If using sweet peppers, remove stems. Quarter
peppers and remove seeds and membranes; cut into 1-inch-wide strips.

3 For seasoning mixture, combine olive oil, basil, thyme, onion powder,
pepper, mustard, paprika, and garlic. Brush prepared vegetables with
seasoning mixture.

4 Preheat gas grill. Adjust heat for direct cooking. Place vegetables on a
piece of heavy foil or on the grill rack (lay vegetables perpendicular to
wires on rack so vegetables don't fall through) over medium to medium-
high heat. Cover and grill zucchini for 5 to 6 minutes; eggplant about 8
minutes; sweet peppers for 8 to 10 minutes; and new potatoes for 10
to 12 minutes or till tender. Turn vegetables occasionally and brush
with seasoning mixture. Makes 4 servings.

Per serving: *257 calories, 4 g protein, 38 g carbohydrate, 10 g total fat
(1 g saturated), 0 mg cholesterol, 13 mg sodium, 747 mg potassium*

Parmesan Buttered Corn on the Cob

Grilled fresh-from-the-field sweet corn is a flavor sensation you won't want to miss.

⅓ cup margarine or butter
2 tablespoons grated
   Parmesan cheese
2 tablespoons mayonnaise or
   salad dressing

1 tablespoon thinly sliced
   green onion
⅛ to ¼ teaspoon pepper
⅛ teaspoon garlic powder
6 fresh ears of corn

1 In a small mixing bowl beat margarine or butter with an electric mixer on medium speed about 30 seconds or till softened. Stir in Parmesan cheese, mayonnaise or salad dressing, green onion, pepper, and garlic powder. Set butter mixture aside.

2 Remove husks from fresh ears of corn. Scrub ears with a stiff brush to remove silks. Rinse ears; pat dry with paper towels. Place each ear of corn on a piece of heavy foil. Brush ears with butter mixture. Wrap corn securely in foil.

3 Preheat gas grill. Adjust heat for direct cooking. Place corn on grill rack over medium to medium-high heat. Cover and grill about 20 minutes or till kernels are tender, turning frequently. Makes 6 servings.

Chive-Mustard Butter: In a small mixing bowl beat ⅓ cup *margarine or butter* with an electric mixer on medium speed about 30 seconds or till softened. Stir in 3 tablespoons snipped fresh *chives*, 1½ teaspoons *Dijon-style mustard*, and ⅛ teaspoon *ground red pepper*. Brush ears with butter mixture. Continue as directed above.

Cheese 'N' Butter: In a small mixing bowl beat ⅓ cup *margarine or butter* and ½ of a 5-ounce jar (about ¼ cup) *cheese spread with bacon* with an electric mixer on medium speed about 30 seconds or till softened. Stir in ⅛ teaspoon *onion powder*. Brush ears with butter mixture. Continue as directed above.

Per serving: 216 calories, 4 g protein, 20 g carbohydrate, 15 g total fat (3 g saturated), 4 mg cholesterol, 196 mg sodium, 203 mg potassium

Curried Fruit Compote

2 medium bananas, cut into
chunks
2 medium peaches or
nectarines, peeled, pitted,
and cut into wedges
2 medium plums, pitted and
cut into wedges
1 large apple, cored and cut
into chunks

¼ cup apricot preserves
2 tablespoons brown sugar
2 tablespoons margarine or
butter, melted
2 tablespoons lemon juice
½ teaspoon curry powder

1 On four 18 x 12-inch pieces of heavy foil, evenly divide the bananas, peaches or nectarines, plums, and apples. Stir together the apricot preserves, brown sugar, margarine or butter, lemon juice, and curry powder. Spoon some of the apricot mixture over each packet of fruit.

2 For each packet, bring up the two opposite edges of foil and seal with a double fold. Fold remaining ends to completely enclose fruit, leaving space for steam to build.

3 Preheat gas grill. Adjust heat for direct cooking. Place foil packets on grill rack over medium heat. Cover and grill for 5 to 7 minutes or till fruit is heated through.

4 Serve fruit mixture over grilled chicken or pork. Makes 4 servings.

Indirect Grilling: Preheat gas grill. Adjust heat for indirect cooking. Place foil packets on grill rack over medium heat. Cover and grill for 8 to 10 minutes or till fruit is heated through. Continue as directed above.

Per serving: 273 calories, 2 g protein, 54 g carbohydrate, 6 g total fat (1 g saturated), 0 mg cholesterol, 72 mg sodium, 574 mg potassium

Curried Rice Pilaf

2 cups cooked long grain rice
½ chopped onion
½ cup mixed dried fruit bits
¼ cup chopped celery
1 tablespoon margarine or
   butter

1½ teaspoons instant chicken or
    beef bouillon granules
½ to 1 teaspoon curry powder
1 clove garlic, minced
⅛ teaspoon pepper

1 In a medium mixing bowl combine cooked rice, onion, fruit bits, celery, margarine or butter, bouillon granules, curry powder, garlic, and pepper.

2 Tear off a 36 x 18-inch piece of heavy foil. Fold in half to make a double thickness of foil that measures 18 x 18 inches. Place pilaf in center of the foil. Bring up two opposite edges of foil and seal with a double fold. Fold remaining ends to completely enclose the pilaf, leaving space for steam to build.

3 Preheat gas grill. Adjust heat for direct cooking. Place foil packet on grill rack over medium to medium-high heat. Cover and grill about 20 minutes or till onion is tender, turning the packet once halfway through. Makes 4 servings.

Per serving: 217 calories, 4 g protein, 43 g carbohydrate, 3 g total fat (1 g saturated), 0 mg cholesterol, 381 mg sodium, 241 mg potassium

Caraway-Cheese Pumpernickel Bread

1 cup shredded Swiss cheese
¼ cup margarine or butter, softened
¼ cup mayonnaise or salad dressing
1 to 2 teaspoons caraway seed
1 16-ounce round or oval loaf unsliced pumpernickel bread

Serve this hearty grilled bread to guests with big appetites!

1 In a small mixing bowl combine shredded cheese, margarine or butter, mayonnaise or salad dressing, and caraway seed; set aside.

2 Cut bread into 1-inch-thick slices, cutting to but not through bottom crust. Cut crosswise down center of bread, cutting to but not through bottom crust (Do not cut crosswise through end slices). Spread cut surfaces with cheese mixture.

3 Tear off a 48 x 18-inch piece of heavy foil. Fold in half to make a double thickness of foil that measures 24 x 18 inches. Place bread in the center of foil. Bring up two opposite edges of foil and seal with a double fold. Fold remaining ends to completely enclose the bread, leaving space for steam to build.

4 Preheat gas grill. Adjust heat for direct cooking. Place bread on grill rack over medium heat. Cover and grill about 15 minutes or till heated through, turning once. Makes 12 servings.

Per serving: *200 calories, 6 g protein, 19 g carbohydrate, 11 g total fat (3 g saturated), 11 mg cholesterol, 300 mg sodium, 181 mg potassium*

Grilled Blueberry-Rhubarb Dessert

Put this fruit dessert on the grill to cook while you're eating the rest of your meal.

3 cups fresh or frozen blueberries
2 cups fresh or frozen rhubarb
½ cup sugar
2 all-purpose flour
½ cup quick-cooking rolled oats
½ cup packed brown sugar

¼ cup all-purpose flour
¼ teaspoon ground nutmeg
¼ teaspoon ground cinnamon
¼ cup margarine or butter
Whipped cream, or half-and-half or light cream (optional)

1 In a medium saucepan combine blueberries, rhubarb, sugar, and the 2 tablespoons all-purpose flour. Cook and stir till thickened and bubbly. Transfer fruit mixture to an 8x8x2-inch metal baking pan or foil pan. Set aside.

2 For topping, in a medium mixing bowl combine oats, brown sugar, the ¼ cup all-purpose flour, nutmeg, and cinnamon. Cut in margarine or butter till mixture resembles coarse crumbs. Sprinkle topping over fruit mixture.

3 Preheat gas grill. Adjust heat for indirect cooking. Place pan on grill rack over medium heat. Cover and grill for 20 to 25 minutes or till topping is set.

4 Serve warm with whipped cream, if desired. Makes 6 servings.

Per serving: 298 calories, 3 g protein, 56 g carbohydrate, 9 g total fat (2 g saturated), 0 mg cholesterol, 101 mg sodium, 281 mg potassium

Grilled Appetizer Pizzas

6 tablespoons pizza sauce
3 6-inch Italian bread shells
1 tablespoon snipped fresh
  oregano or 1 teaspoon
  dried oregano, crushed
½ of a 3½-ounce package sliced
  pepperoni

½ cup sliced fresh mushrooms
3 tablespoons thinly sliced
  green onion
¾ cup shredded mozzarella
  cheese

1 Spread pizza sauce evenly over bread shells. Sprinkle with oregano. Top with pepperoni, mushrooms, and green onion. Sprinkle with shredded cheese.

2 Preheat gas grill. Adjust heat for indirect cooking. Place pizzas on grill rack over medium heat. Cover and grill about 5 minutes or till cheese melts and pizza is heated through. Makes 24 servings.

Mexicana Pizzas: Sprinkle ¾ cup *taco-flavored cheese* over the bread shells. Top with 2 medium *tomatoes,* thinly sliced; 2 tablespoons snipped fresh *cilantro;* and 1 *jalapeño pepper,* chopped (not seeded) *or* 3 tablespoons chopped *green chili peppers.* Cover and grill as directed above.

California Pizzas: Combine 1 tablespoon *olive oil* and 1 clove *garlic,* minced; brush over bread shells. Top with one 12-ounce jar *roasted sweet peppers,* drained and cut into 1-inch-wide strips; 4 ounces *soft goat cheese (chevre),* crumbled; 3 tablespoons sliced *pitted ripe olives;* and 2 tablespoons snipped *fresh basil or* 1 teaspoon *dried basil,* crushed. Cover and grill as directed above.

Pesto, Shrimp, and Dried Tomato Pizzas: Peel and devein 12 ounces medium *shrimp.* Cook shrimp in boiling water for 1 to 3 minutes or till opaque; drain. Chop shrimp; set aside. Spread 6 tablespoons *pesto* over bread shells. Top with cooked shrimp and 3 tablespoons drained and snipped *oil-packed dried tomatoes.* Sprinkle with ¾ cup shredded *Monterey Jack cheese.* Cover and grill as directed above.

Per serving: 59 calories, 3 g protein, 7 g carbohydrate, 2 g total fat (1 g saturated), 4 mg cholesterol, 157 mg sodium, 31 mg potassium

Grilled Quesadillas

These flour tortillas are oozing with cheese and finely chopped dried tomatoes.

¼ cup dried tomatoes
(no oil pack)
1 3-ounce package cream
cheese, softened
½ cup shredded Monterey Jack
cheese

1 tablespoon snipped fresh
thyme or ½ teaspoon dried
thyme, crushed
1 tablespoon milk
6 7-inch flour tortillas
2 tablespoons cooking oil

1 Cover tomatoes with water. Simmer about 2 minutes or till tender. Drain and finely chop. In a small mixing bowl stir together cream cheese, Monterey Jack cheese, thyme, milk, and chopped tomatoes.

2 Brush one side of 3 tortillas with some of the cooking oil. Place tortillas, oil side down, on a large baking sheet. Spread cream cheese mixture over each tortilla on baking sheet. Top with remaining tortillas. Brush the top tortillas with remaining oil.

3 Preheat gas grill. Adjust heat for direct cooking. Place quesadillas on grill rack over medium heat. Cover and grill for 3 to 4 minutes or till cream cheese mixture is heated through and tortillas start to brown, turning once halfway through.

4 To serve, cut quesadillas into wedges. Makes 6 servings.

Per serving: 238 calories, 7 g protein, 21 g carbohydrate, 14 g total fat (6 g saturated), 24 mg cholesterol, 333 mg sodium, 266 mg potassium

Sausage and Cheese Quesadillas

½ pound bulk mild Italian
   sausage
⅓ cup chopped onion
2 cloves garlic, minced
2 tablespoons snipped fresh
   cilantro or parsley

1 jalapeño pepper, seeded and
   chopped
6 7-inch flour tortillas
2 tablespoons cooking oil
1 cup shredded Monterey Jack
   cheese

These meat-and-cheese-filled wedges make a great appetizer or a light lunch when served with a fresh, green salad.

1 For filling, in a medium skillet cook sausage, onion, and garlic till onion is tender but not brown. Drain off fat. Pat sausage mixture with paper towels to remove as much additional fat as possible. Stir in cilantro or parsley and jalapeño pepper; set filling aside.

2 Brush one side of 3 tortillas with some of the cooking oil. Place tortillas, oil side down, on a large baking sheet. Spread some of the sausage filling over each tortilla on baking sheet; sprinkle each tortilla with cheese. Top with remaining tortillas. Brush top of tortillas with remaining oil.

3 Preheat gas grill. Adjust heat for direct cooking. Place quesadillas on grill rack over medium heat. Cover and grill for 3 to 4 minutes or till filling is heated through and tortillas start to brown, turning once.

4 To serve, cut quesadillas into wedges. Makes 6 servings.

Per serving: 302 calories, 13 g protein, 19 g carbohydrate, 19 g total fat (7 g saturated), 38 mg cholesterol, 472 mg sodium, 157 mg potassium

Grilling Charts

Here you go—the griller's guide to time and temperature. Whether you're grilling meat, poultry, fish, or vegetables, directly or indirectly, the convenient charts in this chapter provide the guidelines you need to make things turn out the way you like them.

In This Chapter:

Direct-Grilling Meat

Test for the desired heat (see page 7). Place the meat on the grill rack of an uncovered grill. Grill the meat, uncovered, for the time given below or until done, turning meat over halfway through grilling time.

Cut	Thickness (inches)	Heat	Doneness	Direct-Grilling Time (minutes)
Beef				
Flank steak	¾ to 1	Medium	Medium	12 to 14
Boneless chuck steak	¾ to 1	Medium	Rare	14 to 16
			Medium	18 to 20
Top round steak	1	Medium	Rare	14 to 16
			Medium	18 to 20
	1½	Medium	Rare	19 to 26
			Medium	27 to 32
Steak (top loin, T-bone, porterhouse, sirloin, rib, rib eye)	1	Medium	Rare	8 to 12
			Medium	12 to 15
	1¼ to 1½	Medum	Rare	14 to 18
			Medium	18 to 22
Tenderloin steak	1	Medium	Rare	8 to 12
			Medium	12 to 15
	1½	Medium	Rare	14 to 18
			Medium	18 to 22
Boneless sirloin steak	1	Medium	Rare	14 to 18
			Medium	18 to 22
	1½	Medium	Rare	32 to 36
			Medium	36 to 40
Ground-meat patties	¾ (4 per pound)	Medium	No pink remains	14 to 18
Veal				
Chop	1	Medium	Medium to well-done	19 to 23
Lamb				
Chop	1	Medium	Rare	10 to 14
			Medium	14 to 16
Pork				
Chop	¾	Medium-high	Medium to well-done	8 to 11
	1¼ to 1½	Medium	Medium	25 to 30
			Well-done	30 to 35
Miscellaneous				
Frankfurters, smoked bratwurst, etc.	6 per pound	Medium-high	Heated through	3 to 5
Kabobs	1 (meat)	Medium		12 to 14

Indirect-Grilling Meat

(See your manufacturer's directions for specific instructions on indirect grilling.) In a covered grill, turn off one burner. Test for desired heat above unlit burner (see page 7). For roasts, insert a meat thermometer; place roast on a rack in a roasting pan. Place pan over unlit burner. (For steaks and chops, place meat directly on grill rack over unlit burner.) Cover and grill for the time given below or until the meat thermometer registers desired temperature.

Cut	Thickness/ Weight	Heat	Doneness	Indirect-Grilling Time
Beef				
Flank steak	¾ to 1 inch thick	Medium	Medium	18 to 22 minutes
Boneless chuck steak	¾ to 1 inch thick	Medium	Rare Medium	22 to 26 minutes 26 to 28 minutes
Top round steak	1 inch thick	Medium	Rare Medium	24 to 26 minutes 28 to 30 minutes
	1½ inches thick	Medium	Rare Medium	24 to 28 minutes 28 to 32 minutes
Steaks (top loin, T-bone, porterhouse, sirlion, rib, rib eye)	1 inch thick	Medium	Rare Medium	16 to 20 minutes 20 to 24 minutes
	1¼ to 1½ inches thick	Medium	Rare Medium	20 to 22 minutes 22 to 26 minutes
Tenderloin steak	1 inch thick	Medium	Rare Medium	16 to 20 minutes 20 to 22 minutes
	1½ inches thick	Medium	Rare Medium	18 to 22 minutes 22 to 26 minutes
Boneless sirloin steak	1 inch thick	Medium	Rare Medium	22 to 26 minutes 26 to 30 minutes
	1½ inches thick	Medium	Rare Medium	32 to 36 minutes 36 to 40 minutes
Ground-meat patties	¾ inch thick (4 per pound)	Medium	No pink remains (pork: juices run clear)	20 to 24 minutes
Boneless rolled rump roast	4 to 6 pounds	Medium-low	150° to 170°	1¼ to 2½ hours
Boneless sirloin roast	4 to 6 pounds	Medium-low	140° (rare) 160° (medium)	1¾ to 2¼ hours 2¼ to 2¾ hours
Eye round roast	2 to 3 pounds	Medium-low	140° (rare) 160° (medium)	1 to 1½ hours 1½ to 2 hours
Rib eye roast	4 to 6 pounds	Medium-low	140° (rare) 160° (medium)	1 to 1½ hours 1½ to 2 hours
Rib roast	4 to 6 pounds	Medium-low	140° rare 160° medium	2¼ to 2¾ hours 2¾ to 3¼ hours

Cut	Thickness/ Weight	Heat	Doneness	Indirect-Grilling Time
Beef				
Tenderloin roast	2 to 3 pounds (half)	Medium-high	140° rare	¾ to 1 hour
	4 to 6 pounds (whole)	Medium-high	140° rare	1¼ to 1½ hours
Round tip roast	3 to 5 pounds	Medium-low	140° to 170°	1¼ to 2½ hours
	6 to 8 pounds	Medium-low	140° to 170°	2 to 3¼ hours
Top round roast	4 to 6 pounds	Medium-low	140° to 170°	1 to 2 hours
	3 to 3½ pounds	Medium-low	140° to 170°	1 to 1½ hours
Boneless chuck roast (shoulder, chuck eye, cross rib)	3 to 4 pounds	Medium-low	140° to 170°	1½ to 2 hours
Veal				
Chop	1 inch thick	Medium	Medium	14 to 16 minutes
			Well-done	16 to 18 minutes
Loin roast	3 to 5 pounds	Medium-low	160° to 170°	1¾ to 3 hours
Rib roast	3 to 5 pounds	Medium-low	160° to 170°	1¼ to 2½ hours
Lamb				
Chop	1 inch thick	Medium	Rare	16 to 18 minutes
			Medium	18 to 20 minutes
Boneless rolled leg roast	4 to 7 pounds	Medium-low	160° (medium-well)	2¼ to 3¾ hours
Boneless rolled shoulder roast	2 to 3 pounds	Medium-low	160° (medium-well)	1½ to 2¼ hours
Rib roast	1¾ to 2½ pounds	Medium-low	140° (rare)	¾ to 1 hour
			160° (medium-well)	1 to 1¼ hours
Whole leg roast	5 to 7 pounds	Medium-low	140° (rare)	1¾ to 2¼ hours
			160° (medium-well)	2¼ to 2½ hours
Pork				
Blade steak	½ inch thick	Medium-high	Well-done	24 to 28 minutes
Chop	¾ inch thick	Medium-high	Medium to well-done	20 to 24 minutes
	1¼ to 1½ pounds	Medium	Medium	35 to 40 minutes
			Well-done	40 to 45 minutes
Ham slice (fully cooked)	1 inch thick	Medium-high	Heated through	20 to 24 minutes
Boneless top loin roast	2 to 4 pounds (single loin)	Medium-low	160° to 170°	1 to 1¼ hours
	3 to 5 pounds (double loin, tied)	Medium-low	160° to 170°	1¼ to 2¼ hours

continued

Indirect-Grilling Meat (continued)

Cut	Thickness/ Weight	Heat	Doneness	Indirect-Grilling Time
Pork *(continued)*				
Ribs, loin-back, spareribs	2 to 4 pounds	Medium	Well-done	1¼ to 1½ hours
Ribs, Country-style	2 to 4 pounds	Medium	Well-done	1½ to 2 hours
Loin blade or sirloin roast	3 to 4 pounds	Medium-low	170° well-done	1¾ to 2½ hours
Loin center rib roast (backbone loosened)	3 to 5 pounds	Medium-low	160° to 170°	1¼ to 2½ hours
Rib crown roast	6 to 8 pounds	Medium-low	160° to 170°	2 to 3½ hours
Tenderloin	¾ to 1 pound	Medium	160° to 170°	½ to ¾ hour
Ham (fully cooked) (boneless half) (boneless portion)	4 to 6 pounds 3 to 4 pounds	Medium-low Medium-low	140° 140°	1¼ to 2½ hours 1½ to 2¼ hours
Ham (fully cooked) smoked picnic	5 to 8 pounds	Medium-low	140°	2 to 3 hours
Miscellaneous Bratwurst, Polish, Italian sausage (fresh links)		Medium	Well-done	20 to 24 minutes
Kabobs	1 (meat)	Medium		16 to 18 minutes

Direct-Grilling Poultry

If desired, remove skin from poultry. Rinse poultry and pat dry with paper towels. Test for medium heat (see page 7). Place poultry on the grill rack, bone side up, directly over the heat. (For ground turkey patties, use a grill basket.) Grill, uncovered, for the time given below or until tender and no longer pink. (Note: White meat will cook slightly faster.) Turn poultry over halfway through the grilling time. If desired, during last 10 minutes of grilling, brush often with a sauce.

Type of Bird	Weight	Heat	Doneness	Direct-Grilling Time
Chicken broiler-fryer, half	1¼ to 1½ pounds	Medium	Tender and no longer pink	40 to 50 minutes
Chicken quarters	2½ to 3 pounds total	Medium	Tender and no longer pink	40 to 50 minutes
Chicken breast half, skinned and boned	4 to 5 ounces	Medium	Tender and no longer pink	12 to 15 minutes
Meaty chicken pieces	2 to 2½ pounds total	Medium	Tender and no longer pink	35 to 45 minutes
Turkey breast tenderloin steak	4 to 6 ounces	Medium	Tender and no longer pink	15 to 18 minutes

Indirect-Grilling Poultry

If desired, remove the skin from the poultry. Rinse poultry and pat dry with paper towels. (See your manufacturer's directions for specific instructions on indirect grilling.) In a covered grill, turn off one burner. Test for desired heat above unlit burner (see page 7). Place unstuffed whole birds, breast side up, on a rack in a roasting pan. Place pan over unlit burner. (For poultry pieces, place pieces directly on grill rack over unlit burner.) Cover and grill for the time given or until done. (Note: Birds vary in size, shape, and tenderness. Use these times as general guides.)

To test for doneness, cut into the thickest part of the meat near a bone; juices should run clear and meat should not be pink. Or, grasp the end of the drumstick with a paper towel. It should move up and down and twist easily in the socket. For turkeys and larger chickens, insert a meat thermometer into the center of the inside thigh muscle, not touching bone; thermometer should register 180° to 185°. In a whole or half turkey breast, thermometer should register 170°.

Cut	Weight	Heat	Doneness	Indirect-Grilling Time
Chicken, whole	2½ to 3 pounds	Medium	Tender and no longer pink	1 to 1¼ hours
	3½ to 4 pounds	Medium	Tender and no longer pink	1¼ to 1¾ hours
	4½ to 5 pounds	Medium	Tender and no longer pink	1¾ to 2 hours
	5 to 6 pounds	Medium	Tender and no longer pink	2 to 2½ hours
Cornish game hen	1 to 1½ pounds (whole)	Medium	Tender and no longer pink	1 to 1¼ hours
	½ to ¾ pound (half)	Medium	Tender and no longer pink	40 to 50 minutes
Pheasant	2 to 3 pounds	Medium	Tender and no longer pink	1 to 1½ hours
Quail	4 to 6 ounces	Medium	Tender and no longer pink	½ hour
Squab	12 to 14 ounces	Medium	Tender and no longer pink	¾ to 1 hour
Turkey (do not stuff)	6 to 8 pounds	Medium	Tender and no longer pink	1¾ to 2¼ hours
	8 to 12 pounds	Medium	Tender and no longer pink	2½ to 3½ hours
	12 to 16 pounds	Medium	Tender and no longer pink	3 to 4 hours
Turkey breast, whole	4 to 6 pounds	Medium	Tender and no longer pink	1¾ to 2¼ hours
	6 to 8 pounds	Medium	Tender and no longer pink	2½ to 3½ hours
Chicken, broiler-fryer, half	1¼ to 1½ pounds	Medium	Tender and no longer pink	1 to 1¼ hours
Chicken quarters	2½ to 3 pounds total	Medium	Tender and no longer pink	50 to 60 minutes
Chicken breast half, skinned and boned	4 to 5 ounces	Medium	Tender and no longer pink	15 to 18 minutes
Meaty chicken pieces	2 to 2½ pounds total	Medium	Tender and no longer pink	50 to 60 minutes
Turkey breast tenderloin steak	4 to 6 ounces	Medium	Tender and no longer pink	15 to 18 minutes
Turkey drumstick	½ to 1½ pounds	Medium	Tender and no longer pink	¾ to 1¼ hours
Turkey hindquarter	2 to 4 pounds	Medium	Tender and no longer pink	1 to 1½ hours
Turkey thigh	1 to 1½ pounds	Medium	Tender and no longer pink	50 to 60 minutes
Turkey tenderloins	8 to 10 ounces each (¾ to 1 inch thick)	Medium	Tender and no longer pink	25 to 30 minutes

Indirect-Grilling Fish

Thaw fish or shellfish if frozen. (See your manufacturer's directions for specific instructions on indirect grilling.) In a covered grill, turn off one burner. Test for medium heat above unlit burner (see page 7). For fish fillets, place in a well-greased grill basket and place over unlit burner. For fish steaks and other fish and seafood, place a piece of foil on the grill rack over unlit burner. Place fish on foil. Cover and grill for the time given below or until the fish just begins to flake easily when tested with a fork; scallops and shrimp should look opaque. Turn fish over halfway through the grilling time. If desired, brush with melted *margarine or butter*.

Form of Fish	Weight, Size, or Thickness	Heat	Doneness	Indirect-Grilling Time (minutes)
Fillets, steaks, or cubes	½ to 1 inch thick	Medium	Flakes	4 to 6 (per ½ inch thickness)
Dressed fish	½ to 1½ pounds	Medium	Flakes	20 to 25 (per ½ pound)
Sea scallops	12 to 15 per pound	Medium	Opaque	5 to 7
Shrimp	Medium (20 per pound)	Medium	Opaque	5 to 7
	Jumbo (12 to 15 per pound)	Medium	Opaque	7 to 10

Direct-Grilling Fish

Thaw fish or shellfish if frozen. Test for medium heat (see page 7). Place fish or seafood in a well-greased grill basket. Or, cut several slits in a piece of heavy foil large enough to hold fish or seafood. Grease foil; place fish or seafood on foil. Place the grill basket or foil on the rack directly over the heat. Grill, uncovered, for the time given below or until the fish just begins to flake easily when tested with a fork; lobster, scallops, and shrimp should look opaque. Turn fish over halfway through the grilling time. If desired, brush with melted *margarine or butter.*

Form of Fish	Weight, Size, or Thickness	Heat	Doneness	Direct-Grilling Time (minutes)
Fillets, steaks, or cubes	½ to 1 inch thick	Medium	Flakes	4 to 6 (per ½ inch thickness)
Dressed fish	½ to 1½ pounds	Medium	Flakes	7 to 9 (per ½ pound)
Lobster Tails	6 ounces	Medium	Flakes	6 to 10
	8 ounces	Medium	Flakes	12 to 15
Sea scallops	12 to 15 per pound	Medium	Opaque	5 to 8
Shrimp	Medium (20 per pound)	Medium	Opaque	6 to 8
	Jumbo (12 to 15 per pound)	Medium	Opaque	10 to 12

Direct-Grilling Vegetables

Before grilling, rinse, trim, cut up, and precook vegetables as directed below. To precook vegetables, in a saucepan bring a small amount of water to boiling; add desired vegetables and simmer, covered, for the time specified in the chart. Drain well. Generously brush vegetables with *olive oil, margarine, or butter* before grilling to prevent vegetables from sticking to the grill rack. Test for medium to medium-high heat (see page 7). To grill, place the vegetables on a piece of heavy foil or on the grill rack directly over the heat. If placing directly on grill rack, lay vegetables perpendicular to wires on the rack so vegetables don't fall through the wires. Grill, uncovered, for the time given below or until tender, turning occasionally. Watch grilling closely; try not to let vegetables char.

Vegetable	Preparation	Precooking Time	Direct-Grilling Time (minutes)
Asparagus	Snap off and discard tough bases of stems. Precook, then tie asparagus in bundles with strips of cooked green onion tops.	3 to 4 minutes	3 to 5
Fresh baby carrots	Cut off carrot tops. Wash and peel carrots.	3 to 5 minutes	3 to 5
Eggplant	Cut off top and blossom ends. Cut eggplant cross-wise into 1-inch-thick slices.	Do not precook	8
Fennel	Snip off feathery leaves. Cut off stems.	10 minutes	8
Leeks	Cut off green tops; trim bulb roots and remove 1 or 2 layers of white skin.	10 minutes or till tender; then halve lengthwise.	5
Scallopini squash	Rinse and trim ends.	3 minutes	20
Sweet peppers	Remove stems. Quarter peppers. Remove seeds and membranes. Cut into 1-inch-wide strips.	Do not precook	8 to 10
New potatoes	Halve potatoes.	10 minutes or till almost tender	10 to 12
Zucchini or yellow summer squash	Wash; cut off ends. Quarter lengthwise into long strips.	Do not precook	5 to 6

Nutrition Analysis
Keep track of your daily nutrition needs by using the information we provide at the end of each recipe. We've analyzed the nutrition content of each recipe serving for you. When a recipe gives an ingredient substitution, we used the first choice in the analysis. If it makes a range of servings (such as 4 to 6), we used the smallest number. Ingredients listed as optional weren't included in the calculations.

Metric Cooking Hints

By making a few conversions, cooks in Australia, Canada, and the United Kingdom can use the recipes in *Better Homes and Gardens®* Gas Grill Cookbook with confidence. The charts on this page provide a guide for converting measurements from the U.S. customary system, which is used throughout this book, to the imperial and metric systems. There also is a conversion table for oven temperatures to accommodate the differences in oven calibrations.

Volume and Weight: Americans traditionally use cup measures for liquid and solid ingredients. The chart (top right) shows the approximate imperial and metric equivalents. If you are accustomed to weighing solid ingredients, here are some helpful approximate equivalents.
● 1 cup butter, caster sugar, or rice = 8 ounces = about 250 grams
● 1 cup flour = 4 ounces = about 125 grams
● 1 cup icing sugar = 5 ounces = about 150 grams
  Spoon measures are used for smaller amounts of ingredients. Although the size of the tablespoon varies slightly among countries, for practical purposes and for recipes in this book, a straight substitution is all that's necessary.
  Measurements made using cups or spoons should always be level, unless stated otherwise.

Product Differences: Most of the ingredients called for in the recipes in this book are available in English-speaking countries. However, some are known by different names. Here are some common American ingredients and their possible counterparts:
● Sugar is granulated or caster sugar.
● Powdered sugar is icing sugar.
● All-purpose flour is plain household flour or white flour. When self-rising flour is used in place of all-purpose flour in a recipe that calls for leavening, omit the leavening agent (baking soda or baking powder) and salt.
● Light corn syrup is golden syrup.
● Cornstarch is cornflour.
● Baking soda is bicarbonate of soda.
● Vanilla is vanilla essence.

Useful Equivalents

⅛ teaspoon = 0.5ml
¼ teaspoon = 1ml
½ teaspoon = 2ml
1 teaspoon = 5ml
¼ cup = 2 fluid ounces = 50ml
⅓ cup = 3 fluid ounces = 75ml
½ cup = 4 fluid ounces = 125ml

⅔ cup = 5 fluid ounces = 150ml
¾ cup = 6 fluid ounces = 175ml
1 cup = 8 fluid ounces = 250ml
2 cups = 1 pint
2 pints = 1 litre
½ inch = 1 centimetre
1 inch = 2 centimetres

Baking Pan Sizes

American	Metric
8x1½-inch round baking pan	20x4-centimetre sandwich or cake tin
9x1½-inch round baking pan	23x3.5-centimetre sandwich or cake
11x7x1½-inch baking pan	28x18x4-centimetre baking pan
13x9x2-inch baking pan	32.5x23x5-centimetre baking pan
2-quart rectangular baking dish	30x19x5-centimetre baking pan
15x10x2-inch baking pan	38x25.5x2.5-centimetre baking pan (Swiss roll tin)
9-inch pie plate	22x4- or 23x4-centimetre pie plate
7- or 8-inch springform pan	18- or 20-centimetre springform or loose-bottom cake tin
9x5x3-inch loaf pan	23x13x6-centimetre or 2-pound narrow loaf pan or paté tin
1½-quart casserole	1.5-litre casserole
2-quart casserole	2-litre casserole

Oven Temperature Equivalents

Farenheit Setting	Celsius Setting*	Gas Setting
300°F	150°C	Gas Mark 2
325°F	160°C	Gas Mark 3
350°F	180°C	Gas Mark 4
375°F	190°C	Gas Mark 5
400°F	200°C	Gas Mark 6
425°F	220°C	Gas Mark 7
450°F	230°C	Gas Mark 8
Broil		Grill

*Electric and gas ovens may be calibrated using Celsius. However, increase the Celsius setting 10 to 20 degrees when cooking above 160°C with an electric oven. For convection or forced-air ovens (gas or electric), lower the temperature setting 10°C when cooking at all heat levels.